The Law of Clarity

A Journey of Self-Mastery

Alexandra L. Hindson

Copyright © 2023 Alexandra L. Hindson
All rights reserved. This book or any portion thereof may not be reproduced or used in any manner whatsoever without the express written permission of the publisher except for the use of brief quotations in a book review.

Cover image:
https://www.istockphoto.com/portfolio/1001Love

First Printing, 2023

978-1-7380860-1-6

encreLibre publishing
2019 Riondel North
Riondel, BC
Canada
encreLibre.com

Introduction   1
Chapter 1 – Gaining Elevation   5
Earth   11
Chapter 2 – Mind-body connection   13
Chapter 3 – Gut Brain talking to each other   17
Chapter 4 – Detox   21
Chapter 5 – Mindful movement   25
Chapter 6 – Relaxation   29
Water   33
Chapter 7 – Hydration   35
Chapter 8 – Desires   39
Chapter 9 – Writing down the bones of your life: Journalling   43
Chapter 10 – Vision and Ideals   47
Chapter 11 – Receptivity   53
Fire   59
Chapter 12 – Emotions   61
Chapter 13 – Time: Past, Present, and Future   67
Chapter 14 – Will Power   73
Air   79
Chapter 15 – Breath   83
Chapter 16 – Clear out the Closets   87
Ether   93
Chapter 17 – Silence and Sound   97
Chapter 18 – Mastering the Mind and Our Lives   101
Chapter 19 – Affirmations   105
Chapter 20 – Dreaming   109
Chapter 21 – Presence   113
Chapter 22 – Commitment   117
Chapter 23 – Attention and Concentration   121
Chapter 24 – Communication   127
Chapter 25 – ARDR Sound Healing and Brain Balancing   131
Chapter 26 – Further down the rabbit hole   139
Chapter 27 – A new beginning   143
Bibliography   147

Introduction

Inspired by the teachers who have gone before me, the early and ethical scientists of the East, the sages, yogis, and all the wisdom keepers from around the world, this book has come into being. These sages knew and explored the mysteries of the universe by diving deep into their being, where the Source awaited their arrival. They communed with God and learned about their true nature from their personal experience. Blessed with the open, expansive awareness, they received the key that opened a door into higher dimensions and realms. They returned with well-guarded secrets which they shared with only the initiated, those who had committed their lives in the pursuit of the Highest Truth. They transformed their animal nature, the automaton, bound and controlled by the instincts of survival, physical, mental, and emotional, and found the key to the heart, unlocking Logos, Divine reason, and order of the universe where true freedom resides.

We are both the lock and key to the mysteries of the universe, its origins, and the knowing of it. *The Law of Clarity* is a door to your soul's call to this expansive experience of your inner being and outer world. To open that door requires the courage to use the keys of your inner knowing to unlock the latent powers waiting within. We discover our heart's desire, and when we are clear about what we want and what is getting in the way, the door swings wide open with the magic invocation of our self-awareness. We discover the hidden cave of riches granted by our heart's desire and the courage to seek and persevere when all we want to do is turn back, only to return with the Golden Fleece, the prize of the hero's journey.

I finally said yes to the inner call to embark on this odyssey! I was guided by my Yoga teacher, Swami Sivananda Radha, who had traveled the heroine's journey and returned to help others find their way. She taught me to build and strengthen my character and will to master my instinctual mind. I learned how to create a foundation of wisdom from my life experience while my awareness grew, protecting me from the dangers of moving through a world blind to the inner demons. This book follows my journey of exploration into a deeper understanding of the nature of being through my experience. As a young woman, I was grappling with a seed within that had begun to grow, watered by a desire to understand the secrets of life. Suddenly, "To know is to experience" rolled off my tongue, which has since guided me. I share my personal journey with you, and subsequent new understanding and insights into myself. It is my wish that this resonates with you, the reader, and inspire you to go deeper into your being to find the Truth and purpose of your life.

I use the four elements and their qualities to aid in understanding our minds, from earth to heaven, where we lay the foundation, the ground, and the stone of our self-mastery, building a foundation for the great cathedral of our awareness. Using our lived experience, growing in self-awareness to eventual self-mastery, we rise on the cathedral's steeple, reaching for the heavens. The cathedral's construction spanned multiple generations, much like our journey towards our goals. We start now, and with strong determination, we will reach the inner sanctum of hidden secrets to the higher realms. This book begins with a simple map to those upper realms to gain mastery over nature. We start at base camp and begin by mastering the body, the mind, and the emotions, preparing ourselves to face the obstacles on the journey to the peak. Tested, we will need to retreat for safe ground where we prepare again for the next leg, rising ever upward on the steps of our ability to master our resistance and fear.

Practices provide a simple taste or morsel from a feast of spiritual teachings I have received and been nourished by. Having a teacher at first to guide you forward and a community of practitioners to inspire and support you is helpful. I hope this book will spark a curiosity for a more enlightened way of living in a world that, from one lens, looks 'mad' and, from another, reflects our confusion and pain. We rise out of our perceived limitations, beliefs, and concepts, healed and clear about our true birthright and who we are. When we return with the Truth of our being, we will live in the world with awareness of the possibilities beyond our wildest dreams, and healed, we will heal our world.

Chapter 1
Gaining Elevation

I love climbing mountains. I enjoy the challenge of my physical body, using my will and determination to get to the top for the awe-inspiring views. As a spiritual aspirant, a mountain climber, I needed intense training to navigate the many demons and obstacles on the path that would eventually take me up lofty heights of clarity, inspiration, and awe. It required determination to stay on track, even when there were snowstorms and rock slides, when everything told me to return to base camp. There were times I needed to stop and retreat to get supplies, rest up, and heal from the wounds along the journey to another elevation. I faced fierce creatures of my unconscious who were barring the way to the golden fleece at the top. I learned how to befriend and love them back into my conscious awareness, which required patience, endurance, and fiery determination to rise out of the base instincts where monsters hid in the deep caves of the unconscious. Facing these obstacles required steely courage; they disappeared when I saw them for what they were.

Over the last 25 years, this journey resulted in a sharpened sword of discernment, cutting away the self-protective habits that no longer serve me. I learned to control the compulsive behaviors and ways of thinking clouding my choices, resulting in a clarity of thinking and listening, like the ring of a sacred bell. This clarity would lead me to new, more direct paths. Gone were the familiar ego aspects and obstacles preventing me from arriving at the top of the mountain where I could see in every direction.

In 1997, I was on a steep learning curve when an ego aspect arose. I was in transition from full-time employment to consulting with BC growers and I was avoiding a client and not communicating with him. An inflated ego aspect attracted me to a new business venture, luring me to all the shiny promises of title, travel, and money. I was deaf to the inner voice of my intuition that said, "NO!" Please don't trust the shiny toys and the person offering them. I instead said YES to the too-good-to-be-true offer, ignoring my intuition, resulting in a messy conclusion.

The situation with my earlier client escalated, creating the need for action. Trapped in the spider's web of fear and imagination and the additional revelations that the new client was not acting honorably in their business associations and funding partners, I struggled. The work became unbearable, and I was under incredible stress of my own making. I needed clarification about the consulting I was offering as I had leaped into it without reflection and a business plan. The situation resulted in a climax - I needed to understand what was happening, why, and what action I needed to take. I took a day off to drive to Mt. Baker and climb to the top to get a broader perspective of my life. On this lofty peak, clarity and humility overwhelmed me, and I mapped out a course of right action. I drove home, wrote a resignation letter, and delivered it to my employers the next day. I communicated with my client, who I was avoiding, and we agreed on a settlement to avoid litigation. The following week, a small biotech lab in Seattle offered me a job where I worked with two delightful scientists who were also ministers in the Unity Church. They encouraged me to take the following steps of my spiritual journey: a 3-month Yoga intensive at an ashram, which would intensify and accelerate my climb up the symbolic mountain. This adventure would last over 20 years.

I started longing for clarity at a young age. While transitioning from university in Fredericton, New Brunswick, to Guelph to complete my degree in Agricultural Sciences, I struggled with procrastination and fears of failing, leading me astray from my usual hard-working and committed self. School was more demanding due to all the distractions of living on campus, and I got lost in the glamour and illusion of all the shiny objects of the senses. I had never learned how to manage my time building healthy routines and goals for myself. I was not tapping into my potential as I had yet discovered the keys to success: focus, concentration, and emotional regulation. I needed help with the limitations of my perceptions and clarification about how to change and who could help. I was caught by the wild imaginings of my mind and limited by my interpretations of good and bad, right and wrong, judging myself for my failures, adding more fuel to my pain.

The following year, it began to change. The layers of old erroneous beliefs, fears, and mind-generated perceptions began to soften and many fell away. I found Richard Hittleman's *Yoga: 28-Day Exercise Plan* and committed to a daily self-care practice of returning to my body. Daily Hatha's grounding practice helped me feel calmer, centered, grounded with clarity, with fewer clouds of my deep emotions and feelings. Friends said I looked different, more relaxed, and present. I was finally home, occupying my body more deeply.

My life started to change; it was more effortless and seamless. I got a great summer job in my field of agricultural sciences that eventually turned into a full-time position as a technician managing a university lab and the field research of an alfalfa breeding program. My social life blossomed as I became more confident, connecting more deeply with people, meeting lifelong friends, and connecting with future employers. After graduating to work and travel, I moved to Zurich, Switzerland, exploring this beautiful country with its mountains and four distinct cultures. This experience challenged me to step outside my comfort zone and fears and to move into the flow of each unfolding day, trusting in the journey.

Looking back now, I ask what shifted then to propel me forward, leaping off the fear-based timeline into a courageous place in myself. There were multiple factors, but one that stands out is my commitment to focus on my daily practice of mindful movement, opening up channels of energy trapped in my body at the cellular and tissue levels. I was developing a new awareness of my body and mind, experiencing bouts of clarity, with insights and intuitive knowing that was guiding my life. It was the beginning of the shift of the tectonic plates of my life, opening to more clarity about myself.

This journey towards healing, and clearing away of the clouds of complicated emotions that block the blue sky and sun is what happens when we are curious and long for clear skies, free from the dark shadows of our mental and emotional habits. The healing towards wholeness using spiritual practices is the symphonic orchestration of a beautiful piece of music, where harmony, rhythm, and tempo are playing at the highest frequency. We learn that mindfulness practices can clear the mind of the extraneous clouds and confusion, revealing the peace that awaits in a chaotic world. Like a spiral, this process moves up and down, forwards and backwards, that ultimately takes us back to where we started, transformed. We feel the contractions of life which is constantly expanding and contracting, like the breath, muscles, and minds, tensing and relaxing. The tensing is the willpower needed to act in our lives, and when we relax, we surrender to a Higher Power, allowing us to stretch beyond our limits.

We begin with a glimpse into the human potential, our birthright, rarely encouraged nor spoken of. Instead, we arrive in a world en-cultured with primitive beliefs, limited and separate from each other. Our reptilian brain activates the ancient survival instincts to fight (anger, violence), fright (fear and anxiety), and freeze (withdraw in depression or stop taking action in your life). We are at a turning point in the history of global transformation, and where we land on that wheel will determine who we will be, what we will create, and what our world will look like.

In the historic eastern epic, the *Mahabharata*, during an epochal shift from an era of righteousness and courage to a new epoch filled with evil and unrighteousness, the forces of Light and darkness are at war for the kingdom. There are great and mighty warriors on both sides; the only difference is that on the side fighting for righteousness is Krishna, the Avatar. Krishna is the inner guide, the God who drives Arjuna's chariot, born to fight and win this battle against the dark forces of greed, deception, and disorder. When we turn to our godhead, our inner knowing who guides and directs our lives, and let wisdom drive our chariot, we find the peace, beauty, and joy we have longed for.

As we wind our way together through open meadows, dark forests, mountain trails where we encounter scree or loose rock, steep inclines where we need the help of ropes to help us along, and then to return to where we started, we will be a different person. Like the warrior, our hero of the epic story of mankind, Arjuna, we will learn to shoot our arrows and hit the target of our unique and divine purpose, living authentically and fully expressing our beings. We begin up the symbolic mountain of our bodies, starting at base camp, our feet, supported by the earth. We follow the path of the Great Serpent, from earth to heaven, through the body's energy vortices, starting at ground zero. Where do you want to go on this mountain? What are the obstacles and who will you be when you get a wider perspective of you and your life?

Earth

As Paul Tillich, a twentieth century philosopher and theologian, described, earth is the ground of our being, God, upon which all beings exist, arise out of, and are made of. The earth is the vehicle in which we experience our life. It is the ground we walk upon and live, the Great Mother, and the beauty of Her creation. The earth is solid, symbolized by a square; she is the four corners of the world, the Axis Mundi of our experience. As the earth spins in space, we are a microcosm of the cosmic, and to experience higher states of being, we must first learn the universal principles reflecting our world in the macrocosm. We travel up the mountain from the lower realms of earth, water, and fire to the higher heavens, where the air is thin.

We start at the base, where it can feel heavy with depression, weight gain, tension, etc. Earth is associated with the organs of the large intestine, adrenal glands, and immune system. The ground is the provider of our physical needs, the stability needed to walk confidently with a firm commitment to self-discovery while in this physical realm.

According to Samantha Orthleib, the base or ground of our bodies is where issues such as constipation occur, where the body refuses to let go. The mental and emotional problems that arise from early childhood trauma results in the emotions of anxiety, fear, shame, and victim mentality, with compromised boundaries due to a lack of awareness of what it means to hold a healthy stand for ourselves.[1] We are susceptible to identifying with the victim when we do not stand firm while meeting our needs. We learn how to lighten up and clear our minds and bodies of the excess old baggage of the past that is preventing us from moving forward in our lives and dreams.

---

[1] Samantha Orthlieb, *Opening of the Senses of the Soul, Healing in wholeness with nature's vibrational medicine*, (Senses of the Soul, Canada, 2011), 93

Chapter 2
Mind-body connection

> *"The mind/body connection is like a telephone line - many telephone lines, in fact, teeming with information. Small things like drinking an orange juice with pulp or eating an apple is being received like a telephone call to your genes. Every thought, every thing you eat, every single little thing can tweak your genes activity towards healing."*
>
> — Deepak Chopra

We now step outside our door, leaving home from the familiar comfort, faces, and family members, into a vast world of possibility. It means our routines will change, and the new places will indeed be strange to the mind. The journey of transformation is not the path for the faint of heart, where we will travel into the unknown, returning as strangers to those we left behind. Joseph Campbell, the great mythologist and author of *The Hero with a Thousand Faces*, writes about the call to adventure, "...as apprehended by the mystic, it marks what has been termed "the awakening of the self." We outgrow the familiar life; the old concepts, ideals, and emotional patterns no longer fit; the time for passing a threshold is at hand."[2]

We cross the threshold by removing mental, emotional, and material distractions to return home to the Source. It is the reclamation of the Soul and return of the prodigal son, transformed by experience with a revelation of the oceanic impact of culture designed to build amnesia systems, a deep forgetting of the Truth of who we are.

This awakening took place through a gradual unfolding of memories buried deep in the vehicle of my Soul, my body, and yoga postures like a key opening a lock to the inner temple to liberate the hidden mysteries. I will always remember standing in the Mountain pose before the massifs of the Kootenays in BC, Canada, listening for their secret messages. The

---
2 Joseph Campbell, *The Hero with a Thousand Faces*, (New York, NY: Bollingen Foundation Inc., 1949), 51

asanas or postures were revelatory to the hidden, limiting unconscious memories locked in my body, to rise into my awareness, healing me.

The body is the mother ship of our experience in this 3-dimensional reality. Many secrets are hidden deep within us, and like our earth, we are losing our ability to listen deeply and discover the wisdom that the ancients and the Indigenous peoples have. In our contemporary world, we beat the body into compliance, pushing it, abusing it with poisons, and polluting it with low vibrational thoughts, images, feelings, and ideas both on our own and from the external world. Our "smart" devices accompany us everywhere, feeding us either positive and elevating ideas and talks or, more frequently, mindless chatter that distracts us from our purpose and service. Some of us are at ground zero, vibrationally standing on the precipice of destruction with illness or disease. Yet the crisis is an opportunity hidden in the fire's smoke for profound transformation. My crisis was emotional pain poking me to look at my life, my beliefs, and concepts about myself. The event was a turning point in my life, and I learned I had the power to change the trajectory I was on.

The catalyst was a diagnosis of hypothyroidism, a low-functioning thyroid, so I started cleaning my temple of the physical body. My emotions were creating stress in my life and had taken its toll on the adrenals, then started pulling on the thyroid, weakening it. I could either go on medication for the rest of my life or explore the alternative medical tradition. I chose a neutropath, who put me on an intense program to detox the body, supplementing with vitamins, food, juicing, and other cleansing practices. It required a commitment to focus and discipline myself to change my eating habits. The result was a newfound strength, and when I returned to the doctor, I received a clean bill of health! I learned the body needs time and support to heal and responds well to cleansing, nourishing foods, and using supplements and nutriceuticals.

Sometimes, the call is more serious, demanding deep honesty and courage to face ourselves and our habits. My father was diagnosed at 61 with prostate cancer, and this was his call to the warrior's path, the hero's journey. Fired up with determination to get well, he sought alternative healing practitioners, investing in private facilities where he received treatments that shrunk the tumor quickly by 80%. The prognosis looked good, but the healing stopped when his caregivers confronted him to address his early childhood trauma. He refused, and as a result, the dragon that lurked deep in the unconscious killed him in the end, a toxic unresolved conflict. We begin our healing before the crisis, so our body and mind are malleable, flexible, and strong enough to adapt to the demands of the alchemical process.

We must take responsibility for maintaining our body vehicle. What we feed our body will determine our longevity, productivity, stability, vitality, and creativity. A diet rich in phytonutrients, foods that draw their nourishment directly from the sun, will help keep the mind and body feeling light, clear, and vital. After a recent holiday in Venice and Vienna, I was with my family, who love coffee and sweet pastries. I started to indulge, and by the end of my vacation, I was craving sugar and caffeine. Now that I am back into my routines, I notice a tiredness, distractibility, and indecisiveness I did not have before. The sugar, wheat, and dairy left me feeling heavy, congested, and sleepy. I am now cleansing, clearing, and starving out the desire for sugar to regain my mojo!

Food and hydration are significant in thinking, feeling, and acting. Dr. David Hawkins, an American psychiatrist and spiritual leader, noted that most of his patients suffering from depression were hypoglycaemic. When they balanced their daily meals and reduced or eliminated sugar, the depression disappeared. Our physical health affects our mental and emotional health; we know this. If I wake up with a cold or flu, I do not want to move, think, or do anything. Similarly, if I eat a lot of bread and sugar, I feel tired, lazy, and unmotivated. We need to start with physical well-being to improve our energy and clarity to live more fully.

Due to our current world of corporate agriculture, our food no longer provides the nutrition our body needs, adding toxins and chemical pesticides such as glyphosate, affecting our well-being, often resulting in chronic health conditions such as ADHD, asthma, IBS, and more. The Western world, with our chemical farming disguised food sold by global corporations, poisoned water and air, and a consumer lifestyle, stressing us for more and more what we do not need, have resulted in chronic diseases afflicting our communities, cities, and countries with numbers never seen before. When we take responsibility for our physical well-being instead of the quick fix of a pill of promise that only suppresses symptoms, we feel empowered to make changes in other areas of our lives. We know deep inside us something is amiss, and the change starts there.

Master our Bodies

- Our bodies are like the earth, the mother ship of our experience.
- Detoxing heals the body, but we also need to detox the emotions.
- Food choices and hydration affect our thoughts, emotions and actions.
- Corporate industrial agriculture no longer provides the nutrients needed to maintain optimal health.

Chapter 3
Gut Brain talking to each other

Understanding the relationship between the gut and the brain is critical to healing the body and mind and improving mood, mental health, attention, and concentration. There is an exploding field of research on the role of the microbiome, the micro-organisms of our body, in protecting and helping us stay healthy. It occupies a key position in our mental health, producing neurotransmitters like serotonin and dopamine responsible for happiness, motivation, and self-esteem and acting as a boundary between our outer world and the inner sanctity of our blood. If the gut lining is inflamed, the walls are compromised, releasing toxins into the blood, which can bypass the gut-brain barrier. Several factors influence the health of our gut biome, such as whether we were born vaginally or C-section, breastfed, or fed cow milk in our early lives. Our mothers are essential sources of micro-organisms in our early life, and vaginal birth and breastfeeding inoculate our bodies with a diverse population of bacteria, establishing the community of the microbiome. Other factors that compromise the microbiome in childhood include antibiotics early in life and throughout, trauma and stress, injury, a diet low in fiber, and more. Our earliest beginnings determine our physical and mental-emotional well-being.

Initially, when working with clients, I like to learn more about their gut health. There is much evidence that a healthy gut directly impacts the brain's health and vice versa and operates like a biological feedback system known as a peripheral nervous system. This gut-brain axis is a bidirectional communication system between the gastrointestinal tract, the nervous system, and the brain, which means that each one affects the other, i.e., butterflies in your stomach when you are giving a presentation to your colleagues or when we overeat, especially carbs, we get sleepy.

You will know the saying, 'gut feeling,' associated with a liminal or indirect knowing. As an achiever in your life, work, and school, you will know when you are feeling optimal, you are acting optimally. This whole body communication system, which often starts with the digestive system, will get tangled and confused when one of the operators is not working. Food intolerance is one of the most common culprits, resulting in difficulty digesting and absorbing essential nutrients.

A common antagonist in the body is gluten from conventionally grown wheat. People with gluten intolerance [3] feel noticeably better when they avoid gluten. The extent to which this is true depends on the person since people can react negatively to gluten differently. Damage done by gluten-related disorders results in gluten intolerance symptoms, which show up in almost every system within the body: the central nervous system (including the brain), endocrine system, cardiovascular system (including the health of the heart and blood vessels), reproductive system, and skeletal system. Gluten intolerance can lead to autoimmune reactions and increased inflammation, often resulting in illness. Most of these diseases are undiagnosed food sensitivity. [4]

According to Dr. Axe, symptoms of gluten intolerance or non-celiac gluten sensitivity (NCGS) are widespread and can include:

1. Digestive and *IBS symptoms*, including abdominal pain, cramping, bloating, constipation or diarrhea
2. "Brain fog," difficulty concentrating and trouble remembering information
3. Frequent headaches
4. Mood-related changes, including anxiety and increased depression symptoms [5]
5. Ongoing low energy levels and *chronic fatigue syndrome*
6. Muscle and joint pains
7. Reproductive problems and infertility

---

[3] Gluten intolerance is different from celiac disease, which is the disorder that's diagnosed with someone has a true allergy to gluten. Celiac is actually believed to be a rare disease, affecting less than one percent of adults.
[4] Dr. Axe, Axe, Dr. Josh. "#inflammation at the Root of Most Diseases." Dr. Axe, June 19, 2023. https://draxe.com/health/inflammation-at-the-root-of-most-diseases/

8. Skin issues, including dermatitis, eczema, rosacea, and skin rashes (also called a "gluten rash" or "gluten intolerance rash")
9. Nutrient deficiencies, including anemia (iron deficiency) [5]

Gluten intolerance increases the risk for neurological and psychiatric diseases, including dementia, Alzheimer's disease, and learning disabilities, including autism and ADHD. [6]

Inflammation is the body's natural defense system to maintain bodily equilibrium, such as when the body detects tissue damage or infection, as seen whenever we get a cut, bruise, sprain, or breakage of bones. Problems occur when the inflammation process becomes chronic or persistent without a wound. Chronic inflammation is triggered by reoccurring acute inflammation of an unresolved infection or exposure to chemical and physical compounds. Chronic inflammation leads to symptoms such as fatigue, insomnia, depression, anxiety, constipation, diarrhea, acid reflux, changes in weight, joint and muscle pain, and frequent infections. Most people are unaware of this condition and the needed actions, such as changing diet, removing inflammatory foods, and adding healing foods to our regime. When we don't take the required action, over time, diseases such as diabetes, autoimmune diseases, cancer, depression, arthritis, allergies, and neurodegenerative diseases such as Alzheimer's and Parkinson's disease can develop. [7]

Triggers for chronic inflammation are high intake of sugar and other carbohydrates, transfats, chronic infections, obesity, cigarette smoking, sleep disorders, isolation, and hormonal imbalances such as low sex hormones. [8] The most profound impact on inflammation is stress. When working with a client experiencing acute or chronic stress, we focus on building a mindfulness practice of breath, movement, exercise, meditation, and journaling into their routines. **These are proven practices to build resilience to the challenges of daily life.**

---

5 Ibid.
6 Ibid.
7 Ibid.
8 Ibid.

At this level of the physical, we can take action to reduce inflammation. We gradually cut out all inflammatory foods, including refined sugar, gluten, refined seed oils, deep-fried and processed foods, conventional dairy, grain-fed meat and eggs, and other food sensitivities. Start by eating organic whole foods, and add healthy fats such as avocados, olive oil, flax, and hemp seeds and add anti-inflammatory herbs such as garlic, onion, turmeric, and ginger to your diet, and supplements such as Omega 3, probiotics, zinc, magnesium, Vitamin C, D, E, and selenium. I have found adaptogens such as Asian ginseng, ashwagandha, holy basil, and Rhodiola to be very helpful in supporting me under acute stress. Medicinal mushrooms also help with inflammation symptoms such as Reishi, Cordyceps, and Lions Mane for memory.

Master your Gut Biome

- The health of our gut microbiome determines our mental and emotional health.
- Reduce or cut our gluten, dairy and sugar, which are inflammatory foods that disrupt our gut biome.
- There are foods and supplements to reduce inflammation.

CHAPTER 4
Detox

"Let go of toxic control, in order to regain healthy control."
KAYLA ROSE KOTECKI

We are exposed daily to excess toxins such as heavy metals, pesticides, fire retardants, and more. Our physical environments, food, water, soil, and air are polluted with chemicals such as bromine found in fire retardants and the bleaching agent in flour, aluminum found in excess in our soils, and glyphosate or Roundup in our water, soils, and produce. Fluoride in our water is creating an epidemic of thyroid disorders, while mercury found in old dental amalgam fillings and vaccines contributes to chronic disease. These are a few examples.

Our bodies are intelligent and have natural mechanisms for clearing out toxins. Colds remove toxins through phlegm, and flu, accompanied by a fever, raises the body's temperature to fight infections. When the body is overwhelmed with toxins, serious diseases are necessary to get our attention. With an epidemic of chronic disease in North America accompanied by depression and anxiety, there is growing awareness of what is making us ill.

We are overburdened with toxins and our body needs our help to remove the pressure on our organs, nerves, and endocrine and detox systems such as the lymph, liver, blood, and kidneys. I learned about detoxing the body when I was diagnosed with hypothyroidism in 1993. While working with a neuropath who guided me in cleansing, I removed the toxins in my environment, supporting my body systems with organic vegetable juicing, high-nutrient soups, spring water, herbs, and supplements, ensuring the toxins did not get trapped in the tissues. My body healed, and my thyroid stabilized, preventing me from going on a lifelong prescription of Synthroid.

Heavy metals such as mercury, lead, and arsenic are one of the biggest challenges to the body's healthy functioning. The symptoms of heavy metal poisoning can be subtle and overt, from fatigue, foggy thinking, and muscle and joint pain to nerve damage, memory loss, and spontaneous miscarriage in women. In 2020, after meeting a health coach and visiting her 'clean' home environment, I felt the benefits of their living water and clear air using an air purification system. I decided to clean up my environment and inner terrain, change my diet, remove coffee and alcohol, grow a vegetable garden, and start a 2-year-long liver and heavy metal cleanse. I learned a while back from my herbalist that thyroid problems are due to stressed out and overwhelmed adrenals, liver, and gallbladder. I found a naturopath I trusted who recommended ways to support the pathways of detoxifying the liver, colon/gut, kidneys, and skin. I followed protocols for removing the parasites, which live symbiotically in our bodies, cleaning up the excess heavy metals. I had to start by ensuring my gut was in good shape to manage the release of toxins, then providing optimal drainage systems of the lymph, kidneys, and liver, and then cleansing the metals and parasites.

After an intensive one-month liver and intestinal cleanse, I had more energy, vitality, and a clearer mind. As a result, I went off Synthroid, which I had started taking during peri-menopause. I now use iodine supplements and others to support my thyroid and rebuild the tissue while supporting my liver with supplements, castor oil packs, and enemas.

Cleansing and supporting the body to detox is essential for all of us due to the invasive nature of chemicals in our environment. People who cleanse regularly, 2-3 times annually, and with the changing seasons supporting the body's detox systems rarely or never get sick.

You will know you need to detox if you are:

- Not pooping every day
- Tired and lethargic
- Foggy brain
- Not drinking enough water
- Overweight

- If you experience food sensitivities and digestive issues, allergies, frequent illnesses such as colds and flu, anxiety, depression or severe mood changes, lack of concentration, acne, migraines, headaches, learning disabilities, memory loss, and more.

Practice

Start with an assessment and inventory of your food ingredients, skin care and shampoos, cleaning products, and air quality in your home. Purchase an efficient air and water purification system that removes toxins such as mold, dust, smoke from the air, and fluoride and other toxins from your municipal tap water. Replace your furnace filter every three months and use a HEPA and electrostatic version, which removes dust, mites, smoke, bacteria, etc. I now buy reverse osmosis, remineralized water, and vacuum and dust my home weekly to remove antagonists in the lungs. Review your food purchases, buy organic and local as much as possible, and eat whole foods, shopping outside the grocery store. Better yet, grow some of your food. If you eat meat, buy free-range and antibiotic-free poultry and beef. I started buying free-range beef and noticed a difference in quality, taste, and the feeling of being nourished!

Then, when you start to feel better following the anti-inflammatory diet and previous recommendations in Chapter 3, get an herbal gut/liver cleanse at your local health food store and experience the next level of health and well-being that comes when we take care of our bodies living in a toxic world. The next step on your journey to health is to find a recommended health coach, herbalist, or naturopath whom you trust and who will help you take the next steps on your journey to wholeness, health, and vitality.

Master your Health

- The world is overburdened with toxins in the soil, air and water.
- Our bodies are intelligent and know how to clear out toxins.
- Regular cleansing seasonally supports optimal health and immunity.
- There are clear messages the body gives us when we need to detox.

Chapter 5
Mindful movement

"Yoga is not about tightening your ass. It's about getting your head out of it."

— Eric Paskel

Let's explore the body-mind and the practice of Hatha Yoga, an ancient science that yogis of the past have practiced to heal and strengthen their bodies and expand their awareness. Let's start by stating clearly, Yoga is not about turning the body into a pretzel. Yoga is a science of the self, practiced with any religious belief or personal ideal. Hatha Yoga is the physical practice of mindfulness and meditation, holding the body in postures that stimulate organs, glands, muscles, meridians, and the body's mind, keeping it toned, tuned, supple, flexible, and strong while calming and invigorating it. The regular practice of Hatha yoga starts with a growing appreciation of a strong, lean, and flexible body, which later evolves into an awareness of a quiet inner space of peace. The poses help the body vehicle and its CEO - the mind, chill out, return to equilibrium and equanimity, and function optimally. The practice of Hatha is a self-exploration of the mind-body connection, and people of all ages can use the poses to develop flexibility, strength and poise, contributing to longevity, and youthfulness. Many people start taking Hatha to help with sore backs, hips, shoulders, and more, but when they continue, something surprising develops.

Hatha symbolizes the left and right sides of the body and mind: Ha means sun, the masculine, active, and warm; and Tha means the moon, the feminine, receptive, and cool. When we practice yoga poses, we unite the pairs of energies, bringing harmony to the body. It reminds me of the other two polarities within the brain's two hemispheres, the left and right, which we will address later in the Chapter on ARDR, the brain and heart connection, and the masculine and feminine. Union of the pairs of opposites is the goal of Yoga, and when, for example, the masculine and feminine are dancing together, it is a mystical experience. It is like we are accessing more of our inherent potential of the mind/

body, driving a Maserati sports car in 3rd and 4th gear after years of being in 1st!

It all began in my second year of university when I was experiencing anxiety, creating difficulty in school when I came across Richard Hittlleman's *Yoga: 28-Day Exercise Plan*. As you know due to a committed daily practice of Hatha, a dramatic change had taken place. I was more grounded, calm, and confident, which was apparent to those close to me. I was a different person. From this life-changing experience I have dedicated over 30 years practicing and teaching Hatha Yoga to sustain, ground and strengthen me, and help me stay in touch with what is happening in my body.

This physical practice promotes spiritual wellness and health of the body with the potential to awaken latent powers within to be used in service to humanity. The benefits of a mindful physical practice are many, from gaining a more flexible, youthful body and radiant skin to a calm and focused demeanour to a gradual awakening of the latent power of the body and mind and clarity to the wisdom residing in you. The best way to know the benefits is to experience them! Start with simple stretches and poses you are familiar with, such as neck rolls, arm stretches, shoulder rotations, simple twists, and eye stretches, and rotate them like the hands of a clock. Another is the series of poses called the Sun Salutation, a flow of positions to warm up the body. With daily practice, the Sun Salutation fosters flexibility and helps to build focus and concentration. Excellent sites demonstrate the series, so find one that resonates with you.

Hatha Yoga and journaling have been the key to my healing while helping me build strength and endurance, inner and outer, crystal-like clarity, and physical health and well-being. Using the symbolism of the poses, I have learned from my teacher, Swami Radha, to ask questions related to the pose and then listen to what arises. This dialogue between the mind and body strengthens the bridge between the receptive, intuitive feminine and the active, analytical masculine. It creates harmony in the body, with a rhythm of movement between the physical and the mental. One of the most challenging poses is standing still in the mountain, a simple standing pose. With feet hip distance apart and lengthening through your spine and neck, through the top of the head, stand still with the muscles of the legs engaged. Mountain pose is powerful for stilling the mind or watching it act up, getting very busy as it rebels against the boredom of not doing and the discomfort of being found out.

It was 1998 when I made the arduous move across the country from Ottawa to Kelowna. I left friends, family, a relationship, and a community behind to follow a calling. After a few months of transitioning and starting a new job, I found myself in a yoga class I had never experienced before, with a strange mantra playing in the background and an active inquiry process in the Hatha poses. We wrote down our reflections while in the postures. It was revolutionary. I was unpacking a lot in one class working with one pose and journaling for the entire class. In my first class, while the healing mantra, Hari Om played in the background and I stood in the mountain, I broke down sobbing! I felt embarrassed by my sudden and unexpected emotional outburst, but I was being held by the container of the class, the mantra and the teacher, giving me the protection to feel my emotions. I had finally stopped all the busyness, running here and there avoiding the pain of feeling grief. I started to listen to my body and feelings, allowing the grief of loss to express itself, freeing myself from the tension of pain. My new life now could move forward, free of the emotional clouds blocking clarity.

Ask yourself: How would I describe a mountain using your own keywords. These are some of my keywords: massif, awe-inspiring, overwhelming, courage to climb, still. What are yours? Fear may arise when facing the overwhelming feeling of the mountain as a symbol for an obstacle. These are your symbols for the mountain at that moment. Then, choose one word, stand still, witness what appears in the mind-body as it relates to the word, and write. For example, if you chose overwhelming, you can then go deeper and ask: "What is overwhelming me in my daily life? What action do I need to take to see more clearly and get the answers on managing this more in my life." Stand in the mountain and then see what answer arises. Write it down, and then take action! [9]

Start today and commit to a regular and gentle practice of moving the body with awareness, listening to the messages of your body, and testing them out. Practice adjusting, easing into what is happening in your life, and surrendering to what is and where you want to go.

Master your Body

- The mind and body are connected, when we are more aware of the body we are more self-aware.
- Yoga has several different schools associated with the body, mind, feelings and action.
- Hatha Yoga is a physical practice that brings harmony to the endocrine, skeletal and muscular system.
- Hatha Yoga helps us to listen to our feelings, emotions and body and then to take action.
- You are as young as your spine is flexible.

---

[9] Swami Sivananda Radha, *Hidden Language Hatha Yoga, Symbols, Secrets & Metaphor*, (Kootenay Bay, BC, Timeless Books, 2006), 63.

Chapter 6
Relaxation

Your mind will answer most questions if you learn to relax and wait for the answer.

WILLIAM S. BURROUGHS

Life, our bodies, minds, and relationships all experience an ebb and a flow, a coming and a going, an action and rest, a tension and relaxation. Each moment is a rhythm of both; from this, we create our realities and world out of our thoughts and feelings. We fill each day with activities of the mind and body, and depending on the choices we make each moment, our experience may be tense or calm and a more relaxed approach. Our early experiences of family stress or physical, mental, and emotional trauma remain in our bodies, trapped in muscular tension, holding our energetic potential hostage without our awareness. Along with this are the ever-increasing stressors of modern living, with multiple stimuli from countless sources that fight for our attention. A distracted mind is a tense mind, where our awareness moves in multiple grooves of thinking, stimulating emotions. Negative images, thoughts, and ideas flood the mind, with their resulting feelings undermining the individual's physical well-being with tension and eventually illness or disease. We will experience more vitality and states of joy and peace when we heal and liberate the potential energy locked in our bodies.

The natural, cyclical movement of life, the expansion, and contraction, like tension and relaxation, are like the rhythms of nature, the ebb and flow of the oceans, the rising and setting of the sun and moon, and finally, birth and death. Each day has all three: the birth of the new day, a new you, the sustaining of the life throughout, and then death as we sleep. In deep sleep, the body finally finds relief from the tension of the mind and relaxes completely. Deep sleep phases allow the heart rate to come into a harmonic balance and flow where we return to the Source. We can consciously recreate this experience of deep sleep during the day through progressive relaxation, using our mind's ability to focus and concentrate. We direct our attention to specific body parts (fixing our minds) and suggest the body relax. Repeating this suggestion will magnetize the body part with deep relaxation. As the whole body relaxes, healing can occur as the mind relaxes. The blood circulation is more efficient, the heart rests and slows down, and the breath becomes even and natural. By slowing the body down, the intellect slows down, allowing the intuition to rise into our awareness, that still small voice that requires deep listening to be known. Your intuition is your best friend and will protect you only if you listen and act.

There were times I pushed past and ignored my intuitive knowing to what I thought would bring me happiness. When applying for a position with a potential employer as a biotechnology consultant and lead scientist, I heard my inner voice say when interviewed, "Do not trust her!" I ignored it and accepted the position. I resigned after four months of considerable stress and tension due to their management style. Relaxing the body allows another part of you to speak up, protecting, guiding, and waking you up with fewer hard knocks. When you start practicing progressive relaxation, you begin to calm the monkey mind, and experiencing moments of silence. Suddenly, you have more access to a hidden fountain of wisdom.

Relaxation of the body results in an open and receptive mind. If a student in the classroom is under intense stress from their family or a classroom dynamic or environment, their body will tense up, shutting down their cognitive ability. Due to the release of cortisol from the stress response, this habitual physiological response recreates the memory and reaction of the fight-flight-freeze response. This constant state of hyper-vigilance results in tension that builds up over our lives as we repeat the old historical stories in our minds. Relaxation over time softens the body's muscular system, releasing chronic tension and transforming the individual. We become more receptive and open to listening to ourselves and the people in our lives while building resilience to change. The body and mind become more adaptive to environmental stressors, creating ease, clarity of thinking, and higher feelings such as joy, love, or peace.

Master Stress

- There is a rhythm of tension and relaxation in our lives, our breath and everyday lives.
- Tension holds old unexpressed emotions, that when left unexpressed and released can result in disease.
- Relaxation is related to cognition and access to our inner wisdom.

Practice

Relaxation is an effective practice any time of the day, such as after rigorous activity or Hatha Yoga, where the muscles have been stretched and strengthened with a deeper awareness of the body. You can practice this at work while sitting at the desk or at home before bed. Sit back or lie down, and close your eyes, and practice a visual progressive relaxation for 5 minutes, noting where the tension is arising in your body. The relaxation builds upon this deepening awareness of the habitual places of holding where we can hone in on those areas, repeatedly telling them to relax.

Start by focusing your mind on your body, starting at your feet and moving up the body, suggesting to relax, "Relax feet, relax." Follow up with the awareness of the difference between the relaxed state and the previous tension. Continue up the body to the legs, isolating the muscles of the calves and hamstrings, the pelvis and hips, abdomen, chest, shoulders, neck, arms and hands, and the face, relaxing the tiny muscles of the jaws, cheeks, eyes and forehead. A 10-minute relaxation session will rejuvenate the body, similar to waking after a full night of restful sleep. You may fall asleep, but gradually, upon repeated practice, you will maintain awareness while moving into more relaxed states of being. With continued practice, our awareness expands to make corrections before the misalignment or deepening stress and tension develop into illness or disease. We appreciate the power and effectiveness of the suggestion of relaxing, and its effect on the body and mind.

Water

Our bodies depend on the "elixir" of life, water, to feed our cells, deliver nutrients and minerals, maintain homeostasis, lubricate our joints and skin, and digest our food while flushing our bodies of waste and toxins. Water comprises 66% of our bodies and 95% of our brains.[10] Water is the vascular system of our planet, cleansing and nourishing, contributing to the movement of nutrients that enrich life. In contrast, when a water pipe gets blocked, it builds up and becomes stagnant and putrid. Water at this level becomes toxic. Here is a watery realm, like the Greek god Neptune, ruler of the oceans, who symbolizes the power to master this element. He flows riding his sea creatures, allowing the currents to take him where his will demands. When this element is out of balance, we, like a river when it floods, are overwhelmed by life's challenges. We get lost in the waters of our imagination, creating horror stories or fantasies fed by fleeting images provided by memory, media, culture, and family that take us down twisting and crooked paths. Water is essential if we want total health. This element is associated with addiction or compulsive actions due to imagined desires we have not investigated.

We witness this element playing out in the commercial and consumer world with the compulsive stimulation of desire from the objectification of women as seen in the porn industry, now accessible on your phones with the swipe of a credit card to junk food and sugar available at every "convenient" corner store. The element of water is associated with the sex organs, lower back, kidneys, and bladder. When the water flows through our lives, there is an ease and sense of well-being, vitality, and creative expression. A block of the element or energy may result in many physical symptoms, such as bladder infections or recurring cystitis, and mental-emotional blocks, such as poor emotional and sexual boundaries, guilt, emotional instability, and numbness.[11]

At higher states of consciousness, there is a merging of the masculine and feminine creative forces, creating a new life for the newborn child

---

11 Samantha Orthlieb, *Opening of the Senses of the Soul, Healing into Wholeness with Nature's Vibrational Medicine,* (Senses of the Should, Canada, 2011), 107

or, at another level, a piece of music, a loving meal, or artwork. It is where the sacred masculine and divine feminine merge, which, when lifted to a place in ourselves, is a healthy, balanced, and service-oriented being who dances through life.

Chapter 7
Hydration

"Human nature is like water. It takes the shape of its container."
WALLACE STEVEN

I first inquire when meeting a client about their water intake. Water is essential to cognition and other mental states, such as relaxation, clarity and positive emotions. Dehydration can lead to depression, stress, anxiety, or a combination. Your brain tissues are 95% water, so when you don't drink enough pure water with the essential minerals, it will stress your body. If you are dehydrated, your cortisol levels drastically increase. Under too much stress, the adrenal glands become exhausted, which is essential in regulating the fluids in your body and electrolyte levels. Even 2% dehydration leads to degraded mood, lower concentration, or headaches. Dehydration can result in panic attacks, increased heart rate, headaches, lightheadedness, muscle weakness, and fatigue.[12] Staying hydrated may not stop panic attacks; however, these may become less frequent or diminish with time.

There is a lot of new information arising about water, which can change its chemical structure. The work of Masuro Emoto, a twentieth century Japanese scientist, has studied the effects of vibration on water structure. Using special photographic techniques, he demonstrated the power of emotions, intentions, and thoughts on the structure of water. A positive feeling such as love evokes a crystalline structure that radiates light, while emotions such as anger and shame result in diseased-like images that look like brown goop. Emotions affect the water in our bodies, causing radiant health or disease. Dr. David Hawkins has measured human emotions using muscle testing, the negative and the empowering positive feelings of peace and joy. He found that negative emotions, such as shame and fear, weaken our muscular and meridian systems, while positive emotions, such as courage and love, strengthen us. Let's use an example of the power of emotions to affect the health of our bodies and the waters of life.

---

12 Jillian Levy, *"Dehydration Symptoms: What Happens to Your Body When You're Dehydrated (It's Not Pretty),"* Dr. Axe, August 18, 2023, https://draxe.com/health/dehydration-symptoms/

Media cultivates fear in the collective, incited by the barrage of constant messaging from external sources such as social media, government, the workplace, and schools. Fear shuts down our cerebrum, the home of problem-solving, reasoning, and critical thinking, resulting in blind compliance to the dominant narrative, making us stupid. Words such as "threat, deaths, killing," and the belief that others could kill you if they came close were the messages over the airwaves of legacy media. These words hold a vibration when you think or say them, while words such as health, life, care, and a belief in the body to heal itself are very different. People always get sick, but suddenly, we were afraid we would die. All emotions affect our brain physiology, so our awareness of negative emotions and how to balance them with the positive will help to strengthen our bodies and minds.

Water goes beyond traditional uses, to a more elegant use and understanding of its powerful healing potential within the body. Innovative technology is now available to structure our water into crystalline forms, a hexagonal H_3O, that have demonstrated several healing and health benefits. Vortexing your water helps to restructure it after the chemical and physical water treatments that arrive in your home through pipes that may be eroding, winding through channels that can denature water. When visiting a friend who is a health coach, she and her husband had set up a water purification system that restructured the water into 'Living Water'. I had been using a simple Britta filter on my water, so when I drank their water, my body's cells vibrated with energy and I felt renewed which I had not experienced for some time. The cells of my body were absorbing the structured water more efficiently, resulting in optimal hydration, and the feeling of being deeply nourished. After realizing the impact of water on my health and wellbeing I started to purchase purified and remineralized water.

To maintain hydration add a small amount of Celtic sea or Himalayan salt for their mineral content and lemon to aid digestion while balancing the body's pH. This is also a natural electrolyte drink to avoid the manufactured versions that contain sugar. If you are experiencing a health crisis, investigate the healing power of water and the devices available to restructure water into living water. The Prife iTerra wand is an effective tool and stimulates the body's natural healing processes to help reduce inflammation, improve circulation, and promote relaxation.

Master Hydration

- Hydrating with water, Himalayan salt and lemon provides an electrolyte to reduce thirst.
- Drinking 8-10 glasses of water is considered optimal and reduces stress on the body.
- When we are dehydrated we go into a stress response reducing cognition, contributing to anxiety.
- There are new technologies that restructure tap water back into the quality of spring water, into a healing elixir.

Chapter 8
Desires

> *"Do not spoil what you have by desiring what you have not; remember that what you now have was once among the things you only hoped for."*
>
> Epicurus

From a balanced perspective, desire is neither good nor bad. If we have a desire to be of service or to create something beautiful, it is fulfilling and enriches our lives. Yet, when we are in a constant state of 'wanting' something we don't have, it keeps us in a perpetual cycle of "not having" or scarcity thinking. With this pattern of thought we are affirming to ourselves we are not enough or deserving enough. The 'not having enough' can inflate into greed, a devouring beast, where 'not enough' keeps growing, as a belly expands after gorging a meal, growing ever larger. We want more and more or expect that we should be more than who we are, living a life of quiet desperation with this ball and chain of expectations and the resulting disappointment when it is not achieved. The Buddhists refer to this phenomenon as the hungry ghost, who like the beast above never finds peace in satiation. We have been programmed to want more from the society and culture we are born into. A child raised on the African plateau is encultured by values, beliefs, and attitudes of the tribe very different from our own. As children in the West, we get exposed at an early stage to addictive substances such as sugar, caffeine, and salt initiating the lifelong habits of compulsive eating of sugary treats and caffeine-laden drinks. This may evolve in children into a hunger for more shiny objects, toys, and PlayStations under the Christmas tree. Just watch a children's television station to see what they are programming our children with, so they will crave more sugar, shiny useless objects, entrapping the innocent to want more with the resulting emotions of anger, frustration, shame, and sadness when their desires are thwarted by their parents and caregivers. The taste for more toxic food and meaningless and useless objects starts early.

Recently I have developed a taste for chocolate sundaes with salted caramel ice cream. I have noticed my mind, like Homer Simpson's voice when thinking of beer, sounding my own MMMM for chocolate and sweetness, a clue I am in the early stages of a developing habit. I started visiting the local ice cream shop regularly, satiating the longing for the creamy sundae. I had to stop the habit because I am sensitive to sugar and dairy, so I needed to take action and say NO, and replace it with something more beneficial. I was becoming a slave to the ice cream.

If we keep ignoring the insatiable beast there is a health crisis that wakes us up to a new desire, to be free from our addictive substances and start the process of deprogramming. We now see the man behind the curtain and how it is feeding the corporate state, enriching them while sacrificing ourselves and our children's health and wellbeing. When we learn to separate ourselves from the objects of our desires, the harmful ones, we free up energy from the lower desires, to generate a life of service, offering our unique gifts and skills, bringing joy into your life. It starts with a decision, a cutting away through the power of discernment, and asking, "What will I let go of?" When we release ourselves from the chains of our addictions we can leap into a life reborn into true freedom sharing our unique expression in a world gone mad with consumption.

Master your Desires

- Desires are tricky, being clear about what you desire is key and is beneficial to you and others.
- Clarity about the programs of desire in your life will free you from being on the outside of the wheel of life, and like a leaf in the wind.
- Developing self-awareness is the antidote to taking control of your life, freeing you from compulsive desire.

Practice

What is one compulsive habit draining you of energy such as food (sugar, wheat, dairy, and seed oils are often the culprits), a way of thinking, i.e., a habit of imagining the worst-case scenario or creating catastrophes when facing the unknown, misuse of alcohol, cannabis, or more subtle like an overdoing of an exercise regime like running, that is hurting the body. Take time to name the habit, i.e., living without it will disrupt your life. Reflect on when it started. What was the trigger? What in your life are you avoiding, using the habit to protect you from the discomfort of facing it?

Chapter 9
Writing down the bones of your life: Journalling

"Whether you're keeping a journal or writing as a meditation, it's the same thing. What's important is you're having a relationship with your mind."

NATALIE GOLDBERG

I have had a regular writing practice for over 35 years now, writing down memories of dreams, and aspirations and during challenging times. I began a more intensive journalling practice 23 years ago while studying yoga. I found that keeping a journal and expressing my feelings on paper unleashed revelations about my life that catalyzed a change in my mindset and choices. Expressing uncomfortable emotions of anger, joy, sadness, and fear has immense benefits in addressing the daily repetitive irritations and problems. When we write them in a journal, we allow ourselves time to digest and accept what is. Soon you will observe and experience that indeed you have the power to change yourself and your life situation, and what seemed confusing is now clear and the action needed is apparent. Where you were once discouraged, a sense of hope grows, and you realize you can do something about it. This strength never before suspected in yourself provides the will to take responsibility, take action, and keep going when all you want to do is give up. Ideas of "I never will be able to do this," become "I will try." To "Yes I can!"

My own experience began when I picked up Julia Cameron's *The Artists Way, A Spiritual Path to Higher Creativity*, at a time when I was experiencing difficulties in my romantic relationship. The practice of 'Morning Pages' was the beginning of the shifting of the tectonic plates taking me on the exciting but difficult journey of healing. I rose every morning and hunkered down in my writing nook of glass all around me, like a tree perch, and wrote for 20 minutes, 3 pages without stopping, creating an atmosphere for a stream of consciousness to flow. I wrote my heart out so to speak, expressing the difficult emotions I was experiencing while in a relationship that was triggering past childhood trauma. I was invoking the goddess with me to take charge of my ego personality that was creating havoc in my life. I was being initiated into the unknown, a hero's journey that led to a solo car trip with my dog to New Mexico. A creative muse or genii was evoked, and I was painting, visiting art galleries, and meeting wise, and spiritual people who were on a similar journey. I read poetry by Rainer Maria Rilke and pondered the meaning of life. More importantly, I was getting a clearer picture beyond the clouds of my emotions that were beginning to part, revealing a blue sky.

This clarity comes slowly, as we process the layers of emotions that have built up in the mind and body over the years. The commitment and willpower to write daily will act as a ballast, as found in the ship, balancing the heavy weight of past experiences and trauma. The practice of daily reflection allows you to observe the patterns of thinking that create procrastination with thoughts of, "I can't do this, it is too hard" or "It is boring or I am bored, let's take a break and wait until tomorrow." The practice of daily reflection strengthens the observer mind, a kind of objective witness to our thinking, who catches the fish, darting here and there, hiding from our awareness. We are given a power, the Power to Choose what we want or do not want to create in our lives.

There are many ways to journal and each one has powerful benefits from manifesting your dreams to building better communication skills. Journalling offers blueprints for your goals and dreams in your life while teaching you to be more present with yourself, building a desire to know yourself. Use the journaling practice to heal from emotional stress, anxiety, and depression. It will also unlock your creative potential using a stream of conscious writing, giving you freedom to flow without criticism. The outcome of journaling is building confidence because when we relive a positive experience by journaling about it, it boosts serotonin and dopamine levels.

Master your Life

- Journaling, writing our thoughts and feelings regularly brings clarity, awareness and conscious action.
- Journaling strengthens the observer mind, creating detachment from the external circumstances.
- Through journaling we take back our authority from the external authorities, discovering our authentic voice.

Practice

How to journal: You can use a bullet journal, record on your phone or tablet, use an app, or handwrite in a journal or notebook. There are benefits of the experience of handwriting, slowing us down to connect to our emotions and removing the inner critic who wants to go back and correct the red underlines when computer generated.

Get yourself a notebook or journal that inspires you. You can write stream of consciousness, writing whatever comes to your mind without editing.

Ask yourself questions to help you focus or shift a bad mood, such as: What am I grateful for today? What were my victories? What was my most significant learning? A moment I appreciated today? Or ask how am I? Physically? Mentally/Emotionally? Spiritually?

Review your journal regularly, look for repetitive thinking and feeling, and ask what needs to change. You may notice you complain about the same situation daily, a conflict with a friend, colleague, or teacher. If so, ask, "What action do I need to take to bring harmony and shift my thinking and feeling about this situation?" Then, brainstorm ideas. You may want help or support from a professional such as a counselor, or coach to find helpful ways to work with difficulties arising in your life.

Journal your goals and dreams for your life, for the next six months, one year, 5 or 10 years! Remember, life is short, so ask yourself: What is my life's purpose? And by reflecting on this, you will develop and find meaning in your life.

CHAPTER 10
Vision and Ideals

"The only thing worse than being blind is having sight but no vision."

HELEN KELLER

I have been sharing this practice with hundreds of clients who are students, entrepreneurs and in personal development workshops. I ask them if they have a vision or a goal for the next 4 months, 6 months, a year, or more. All of them say no and I am often surprised. If you were traveling to a place you did not know how to get to, would you leave home without a map, a compass or your digital GPS? Most likely not unless you are a homing pigeon or completely trusted your intuition to guide you. Many of us have never learned about setting a clear path for where we want to go. Most often we have no idea where, what, how, or why we are doing what we are doing. If you are not clear why you are embarking on a journey most likely you will not have the motivation to get there. If you do not have a map, you will most likely get lost, and waste a lot of your precious time and energy trying to find your way. Curiosity about our direction in life, we set off on a journey for clarity, to learn how to navigate life, ourselves, our strengths and weaknesses, and what needs changing. The early journey ideally would start in childhood, but our school system is more interested in filling our minds with limiting beliefs and concepts and less exploring them.

I started my journey of discovery at 23 on a work exchange in Switzerland. Before that, I had left my hometown of Oromocto, NB to complete a science degree in agriculture at the University of Guelph. Even with so much stepping out into the world, I was still timid, unconfident, and anxious. After starting to practice yoga and initiating a shift, a longing for a greater adventure emerged so after graduating I found a program where I could work abroad in my new field of agriculture. I left for Zurich, Switzerland days after my graduation where I worked for several months with a graduate student at the ETH, a university of science and technology. I traveled by train every weekend to explore and climb mountains and then traveled for a couple of months afterward to other European countries. This was a time of stepping out on my own into the unknown, navigating trains and planes, hostels, planning my itinerary, and finding and locating art museums, restaurants, and grocery stores. I had to pull up my bootstraps and learn how to find my way in a new world. Freedom and confidence grew in me as I succeeded in straddling the hurdles along the way. This is where I began to journal about my experiences and feelings and developed a love for photography. I returned where I had begun, changed, and as a friend described, the butterfly had emerged from the cocoon.

Self-exploration is a necessary part of the journey towards a clear vision. If I had known more then about visioning and getting clear about what I wanted to unfold during my experience, using affirmations, my experience may have yielded even more rewards. The vision or map can be a sketch starting with the qualities you want to develop in yourself and unbeknownst to me I had cultivated courage and the confidence to face the unknown. After returning, I landed a position with Crop Science, at the University of Guelph, and was eventually promoted to lead technician for the forage breeding program. The experience in Europe gave me the confidence and courage to step into a role traditionally filled by men. I learned to operate precision seeders, large equipment tractors, and trailers, and lead a team of summer students by the age of 25. Eventually, I moved to Ottawa where a former employer offered me a position with the alfalfa breeding program with Agriculture Canada. I had learned the art of leaping into the unknown, and discovered the universe love leapers!

We easily ignore the richness of our past, whether it be filled with adversity, good fortune, or both, the two sides of the same coin of our life. My hero Arjuna fights for righteousness and justice, while between the two opposing armies he is accompanied by Krishna, the godhead, who teaches him that there is victory in defeat and defeat in victory. I have heard so often from people who have faced great losses that it was the best thing that happened to them as it taught an important lesson.

The practice of a life review helps to look back and harvest the gems of your life experience, the gold hidden in the hillsides of your early life experience. For example, when I turned eleven, transitioning into a new life without my father, living in a small apartment, I loved planting flowers. When we moved to Fredericton, NB from London, ON I was shocked by the change of living in a middle class home and loss of my father, I dug through the grass into the earth and created a bed of marigolds, the color of the sun that brought joy to my tender heart. I did this in our next home, creating more gardens, and planting more flowers. This memory and experience was an expression of my soul and explains why I value the natural beauty in a flower, a forest, a mountainside, or an ocean. This informs what is important to me, and what I need to ensure is present in my life, actively feeding my soul as often as I can.

Create your life with a vision

To envision is to hold an image of your choosing that you wish to create now in your life. It is a call from the heart! When I was in a major transition in my life and I felt powerless and depressed, I reached out to my spiritual teacher. I explained what I was feeling and her brilliant and succinct question was, "What is your heart's desire?". I immediately replied, "Travel!" This was a call from my soul, and I heard it at that moment. My mood lightened and I created my next step, which was a European adventure the following year, 2008. In the meantime I traveled back in history to my previous home in Ottawa, visiting old friends, and seeing how I had changed after nine years of intensive yoga training. It was a profound experience, helping me to get clear about my next steps and to remind me what I value, friends, family, beauty, integrity, and honesty. I began to envision my journey to Europe and eventually, it took a life of its own, unfolding into a photo journal project, a journalist's pilgrimage to experience the Gothic Cathedrals I had taught in darkened classrooms for 6 years as an art history instructor. Now I was photographing them myself, capturing my personal experience of the sacred architecture, and using my yogic practices for a deeper experience. The preparation for the journey kept unfolding, as I planned out the where's and when's, and who I wanted to visit. It then turned out that my uncle was to be in Paris at the same time. Synchronicities were everywhere! I knew that my vision, the intention, and the attention I was giving it gave it a life of its own. I had surrendered the vision and was living in the flow with a rhythm of my life, the Tao, "a cosmic tapestry in which each of the threads is seamlessly woven into the whole."[13] My intention of meeting and speaking with church leaders resulted in similar synchrony of timing, where by chance I met the Archbishop of Canterbury in a Sunday morning gathering and asked an important question I was holding in my heart, *What about Mary?*, which developed into a blog of articles about my co-creative adventures with the Divine Feminine, the powers of manifestation.

Life Mission

Reflect and write your life mission starting with your roles in your life, i.e., student, friend, daughter/son, husband or wife, career position, and identify your ideals for each. For example Steve Covey, in his book, *The 7 Habits of Highly Effective People*, uses this example:

Mission Statement: My mission is to live with integrity and to make a difference in the lives of others.

To fulfill this mission:

I have charity: I seek out and love each one regardless of their situation.

I sacrifice: I devote my time, talents, and resources to my mission.

I inspire: I teach by example that we are love and can conquer our obstacles.

I am impactful: What I do makes a difference in the lives of others.[14]

---

14 Stephen R. Covey, *The 7 Habits of Highly Effective People*, (Simon and Schuster Ltd., 1989), 136.

Each statement is a directive to the subconscious mind, clear in its brevity, and inspiring to the heart with feeling words, such as love and devote. The feeling is essential to our ideals and their manifestation as it is the energy and rocket fuel to get you to your destination. When you decide what you want to create, and who you want to become in the life domains such as mother/father, relationships, friendships, work, business, money, etc., this will provide a clearer path for making decisions on a daily, weekly and monthly basis and will give you the words, ideas, and images for the journey.

Use the SMART goal approach to guide your process: Be Specific (simple, sensible, significant), make it Measurable (meaning, motivating), Achievable (agreed, attainable), Relevant (reasonable, realistic, results-based), and Time-bound (time-based, time-limited/cost limited, time-sensitive)

Most of us long for a way of life that expresses who we are in full expression of our life purpose. Getting clear about who you want to be, where you want to go, and how you are going to get there is the first place that we start, a map to guide your choices, actions, and words. Getting clear about how you would like your year, a project, or a dream to unfold gives you the confidence and clarity for what you need to do. When we are clear about our ideals, or vision of our lives, we move forward with more confidence and courage.

Identifying your ideals is the most important first step when starting a project, getting married, choosing a career, or building a business. This process helps you get clear about who you are, why you have chosen the current path, what your values are for yourself, and more. This process allows you to set powerful intentions about your ideals, your social and family life, the skills you want to develop, and the service you want to give to the world. According to Victor Frankl, author of *Man's Search for Meaning*,[15] a 20th C seminal testimony of a man's experience of surviving Nazi concentration camps, aiming high will get us to where we want to go, so aim higher than you think or believe about yourself, and you will arrive where you are meant to be.

While completing a graduate degree in Education in 2015, with a focus on Creativity, Sustainability, Self Realization, and Well-being, and counselling university students in academic and life strategies, I was experiencing peak moments, an expansiveness due to the inspiration of my instructors and my love for learning. I would walk in reverie in a park near the University of Calgary campus after classes in creative writing, and student presentations on the writings of Dr. David Hawkins and Sai Baba. My school colleagues built deep and meaningful ties due to our shared inspired moments of personal insight.

One semester, after teaching university students the art of visioning and goal setting while aiming high, I decided to practice what I taught. I set a goal and vision for an A+ in my courses. I had a history in my undergrad years of underperforming, so an A+ was a rare experience. That semester with great surprise I received my first A+, and suddenly my perception of myself as a student changed. I was now capable of achieving what I envisioned, using a clarity of knowing that it was possible. I watched as I started to act the part of a confident and successful student, planning, organizing my assignments, and going the extra mile with a commitment to my success. I now knew from personal experience the power of a vision.

Master your Future

- Visioning and goal setting are our compass for the future
- When we use the power of our imagination in a positive and directed way, we create what we want.
- The energy of the vision is the feeling behind it, the rocket fuel for lift-off towards your destination.
- Aim high when setting out your goals, just enough to shift your perception of yourself.

---

15 Viktor Frankl: *Why believe in others / TED Talk*, September 20, 2023, https://www.ted.com/talks/viktor_frankl_why_believe_in_others.

Chapter 11
Receptivity

"The ego is the eggshell and you will have to come out of it. Be ecstatic like the newborn bird as it flies into the sky. Get out of all protections and shells and securities. Then you will attain to the wider world, the vast, the infinite. Only then do you live, and you live abundantly."

Osho[16]

Receptivity may be a word that conjures up feelings of vulnerability, tenderness, fear, and an assertion of independence, rejecting help from others. What does it mean to be receptive and open to receiving from another? I grew up as the oldest in a single-parent family, where I had to learn to take care of my brothers, especially my youngest brother who was only 4 months when my father left the family unit. It never occurred to me to ask for help because of the pride I had in the belief in my independence and strength. I learned to carry a lot of responsibility that was not mine for the love of my family. This has gotten me into situations where I took on responsibilities or the burdens of others that were inappropriate, resulting in emotional pain. These people, authority figures, and systems have been my teachers of what happens when we don't take care of ourselves first, before offering help to others.

Many years ago when I was teaching art history at a community college, I was preparing the slides and notes when a security guard knocked on the door and said, "I need your help." His voice was resonant with sincerity and humility. This was etched in my memory because he was demonstrating vulnerability to a stranger. I was moved and realized there was strength and courage needed to make this request. Vulnerability is a strength and a willingness to face the unknown.

Recently I developed a severe bladder infection. I treated it with natural remedies but it persisted to the point that I developed a fever in the

---

16 Osho, *Courage, The Joy of Living Dangerously*, (New York, NY, Osho International Foundation, 1999) 128.

afternoon and was bedridden for the rest of the day. I had no energy to make meals or eat, and I was not getting better. I gradually got so weak, that when I met on the phone with my herbalist she recommended I call in my friends and ask for help! It had not occurred to me to ask for help. As I reached out there was an old fear that my call for help would be ignored. Instead, a friend arrived and immediately hopped into preparing food, making soup, and more. Another came with her deep love and compassion for others and simply sat with me, so welcome at a time of physical weakness and illness. If you believe that, "I can do this by myself," accompanied by, "I can do this better than anyone else so why would I ask another for their help" and it will protect you is a prison of the hard shell of the ego. When a friend comes and knocks on this locked door, they cannot enter.

Our world when we look around is born out of interdependence, from the two parents of the newborn child who is brought into life, to his or her extended family, and to the community that raises the child. A grove of trees we now know communicates through their root systems, supporting and providing necessary nutrients to one another when stressed or weakened! We have forgotten our natures as social beings who depend on the family and the community, allowing others to come in and touch our hearts. Courage is needed to say yes to life, which is overflowing with the unknown, the dark where we have no control but to leap and trust in our true power within.

The risk we take to be vulnerable in our lives is a gift to others to practice generosity and compassion. One of the greatest gifts I received was when my mom came to live in my home city where she could live in a community where unique professional supports were in place for seniors who were diagnosed with dementia. While living alone in a northern community, Mom began to isolate herself especially after her driver's license was taken away after failing the annual exam. I was resistant at first when my brother suggested we move her to Calgary, believing I would lose my "freedom" due to the responsibility of caring for her needs outside the professional support, and the unknown of what lay before me. After moving her I found such joy in witnessing her happiness being in her new community where she made friends with the residents and staff and enjoyed singing and walking with others, playing games along with multiple coffee breaks with people who she could talk to. The years I had with her gave more meaning to my life as our relationship bloomed into a friendship, sharing meals, walking, and being in nature, together. There are many memories of the joy we shared as we drove into the beauty of the mountains, having High Tea at the Banff Springs Hotel, to holding her hand, sitting in silence with deep presence and reverence in the last days of her life. The gift of dementia for her was to let the critical mind recede into the background allowing for her essence, a beautiful, loving woman who many came to love, even the nurses in those last days of her life. I grew to appreciate, instead of resenting her for the small infractions I condemned her for, who she was, and what she had accomplished, raising three children as a single parent, while working a full-time job ensuring we were well dressed, fed, and loved. She lived a life of service in the church, to her family, caring for her grandchildren in her golden years, a remarkable life of generosity and unconditional love.

When we open ourselves to another, instead of protecting ourselves and holding back, we commune with each other, meeting each other in the heart. Yet, the heart has to first soften and open to ourselves, where mercy, love, understanding, and compassion reside. We take time to sit with our tender hearts, our feelings, and emotions, accepting them and loving them into new life. We become vulnerable to ourselves first, discovering who we are, and building faith and trust in our authentic beauty. We let go of the critical perfectionist, the hard metallic feel of the intellect, who demands and protects us from the inner tyrant raised on the beast of a system of education that keeps reminding us we are not enough.

How do we come back to this uncritical childlike quality who is open to life, without the dark filters of judgment, criticism, fear, etc.? We can start now and as Christ said: "Enter the Kingdom, Become a child; Become a child, Enter the Kingdom".[17] How do we return to this innocence? Is it about remembering who we are? As children, we are closer to our essence, in tune with it, unencumbered from the vicissitudes of the tribulations of time. As a child, my mind was not occupied with the stressors I have as an adult. With more responsibilities along with cultural pressures, we succumb to the subsequent expectations of society, family, friends, and church. Some of us are wearing layers and layers of clothes that weigh us down with multiple ideas and beliefs and their accompanying emotions. For example, ideas and beliefs about perfection will be accompanied by shame, disappointment, guilt, fear, and anger. To become like a child, start by removing the layers of heavy coats you have used to protect yourself.

Start by addressing the emotion, which acts like an alarm signal to our feelings about a past or present event. Observe where it shows up in your body, the effect on your mood, and how the heart rate changes, for example, the burning feeling of anger as it chokes your expression, blinding you in the moment. Then there is sadness or grief and the heavyweight in the center of our chest or fear that may, depending on the trigger, block our throat, like the dreaded nightmares when you are frozen in body and voice, trying desperately to yell or scream for help. Stay with the emotion, while removing the story associated with it, observing what is arising. Experience the vulnerability of the moment, the feeling and allow it to be freed from the body.

It is the chronic expression of these difficult emotions that has resulted in a multi-million dollar industry of drugs, that we seek out for temporary relief and to lighten the heavy burden of our load. **In NA approximately 120/1000 people are on anti-depressants.**[18] Our culture has taught us to repress emotion and to seek a quick fix outside ourselves, a belief cultivated by the culture that feelings of calm, happiness, joy, bold, courage, etc. can be found in a bottle, a relationship, the newest outfit or object or in more subtle instances of escaping to the latest spiritual retreat. Yes, there is spiritual addiction when we seek happiness that awaits within, on the outside in a guru or

---

18 Sussex Publishers. (n.d.). *An epidemic of antidepressants.* Psychology Today. https://www.psychologytoday.com/us/blog/out-the-darkness/202003/epidemic-antidepressants

spiritual community.

My own experience with this was when studying yoga in a community, a greenhouse for growth and awareness. The egoic aspects showed up in vivid technicolor while some evaded and kept me in a loop of fear and timidity. I put my teachers on pedestals, creating even more separation, and closing me off from my true spiritual birthright. I often walked on tiptoes around them, afraid to be seen, because I knew they saw my real, vulnerable self. Pride was an obstacle to being honest with myself about the glaring low self-esteem and perfectionism, ideas of what and who I was supposed to be as taught by my family and culture.

I was determined to heal this and my inner Knowing was there to guide me. The community of teachers and the Yogic teachings taught me tools and practices to heal, to reveal, and to release from my physical and energetic body the pain of trauma creating a defensive mechanism that kept me locked in the walled up world of self-protection. I opened myself to the emotions associated with painful moments and sat with them, feeling them, raging against the absent father and critical mother. This was followed by the tears and like the storm that passeth, a great calm followed. I could now see my father and mother with new eyes. I was no longer the victim of their wounded egos and instead like superwoman, I shed the heavy layers of the cape and flew above the conditions and saw them from a higher view, with clarity, understanding, love and compassion. I was freeing myself from the multi-generational conditioning and belief systems.

Our belief systems create the paradigm that can lock us in a box with walls high enough to block our view of what is real, preventing us from removing the fashionable rose-tinted glasses. This box is based on a collective set of values, such as the belief in scarcity, in a small limited self, who is separate from the world. We need to free ourselves from the collective archetypes of father government (authority) and mother indoctrination systems of education and health, who like my parents unintentionally acted from their gaping trauma wounds. One of the most transformative practices I learned from my teachers is a visualization of Light, where I would see myself opening to the Light penetrating my body and cells. [19]

> Practice: Positive use of your imagination.
>
> See yourself in your imagination as brilliant white light enters through the top of your head, filling you from your feet up until your form is overflowing with this light. See yourself transparent without the familiar image of your body. Now, you are a mass of light. This practice helps us to identify with something greater and vaster than our limiting beliefs and concepts, which have kept us in our boxes of blindness to our potential.

Master Receptivity

- Receptivity is a form of vulnerability, a risk we take when we ask for help from another.
- Giving and receiving are mutually dependent on one another.
- Perfectionism blinds us to our needs and the tender emotions of our heart.
- If we cannot receive how can we hear the call to change, heal and transform ourselves and the world.

---

[19] Swami Sivananda Radha, *Kundalini Yoga for the West, A Foundation of Character Building Courage and Awareness*, (Kootneay Bay, BC, Timeless Books, 1993), 104.

Fire

Fire is the element of both creation and destruction. A forest fire cleanses the dead fallen trees, allowing new growth to emerge. Pine cones need the heat of the fire to open and seed the forest! Fire is dangerous as it takes life and wounds the body. We know when something is hot as our nervous system reacts, and we pull away, a physiological response that protects us. Yet, the fire of our stomachs digests our food to make nutrients available to the rest of our body.

The sun's fire gives life to all things, and it's light, the source of all, shines down on us with no preferences. The ancients worshipped the sun, recognizing that we would not experience a world without it. The light of a candle shines in the dark places of our minds, illuminating the cobwebs, the yucky creatures lurking in the shadows. Fire is also an emotion that can burn away our reason; emotions such as anger, resentment, jealousy, envy, and pride can cause us to lose our humanity, fall into our animal instincts, and act mindlessly and without reason or logic. When we learn to hold the fire and use it to burn away our negative aspects, we are in touch with our true power, the power of will. Anger directed toward positive action is a reckoning force.

Passion, another fire, can blind us, especially in a moment of loss of reason, or take us to great heights, such as a passion for justice, truth, love, beauty, art, the word, to great works of literature, art, and music. Depending on the degree of the desire, passion for a higher elevated way of being is the beckoning call from the lighthouse of the soul to discover the truth.

The organs of digestion are where health issues arise in our bodies, such as difficulty digesting our food and our experiences, accompanied by the mental and emotional problems of addiction, anger, depression, control, worry, and resentment. The symbolic powers of fire are vitality, self-worth, spiritual strength, leadership, and empowered will.[20]

---

20 Samantha Orthlieb, *Opening the Senses of the Soul, Healing into Wholeness with Nature's Vibrational Medicine*, (Senses of the Soul, 2011), 123-124.

Chapter 12
Emotions

*"But feelings can't be ignored,
no matter how unjust or ungrateful they seem."*
ANNE FRANK, THE DIARY OF A YOUNG GIRL

Emotions are the fuel that fires our life. Our emotions can support or aid our self-development, improve our ability to manifest our dreams, the clarity in which we experience our world, and the flourishing of relationships. It is the fuel for our vehicle, our rocket-ship, to lift us off the earth, defying weight and gravity. We can consciously use and direct positive emotions towards our ideal and our vision for ourselves. Cultivated positive emotions such as love, joy, and courage are expansive. Dr. David Hawkins states positive emotions strengthen our bodies and minds, "Aligning with a strong, positive attractor field rather than the weak linear ego."[21] Success in all areas of our lives is inevitable when we cultivate positive emotions and build and strengthen our character.

To influence others, one must cultivate positive emotions and an unblemished character. What does character mean? According to Swami Sivananda, character is power; where knowledge is power, knowledge is impossible without character.[22] It is an ideal I want to cultivate in myself. I often see qualities in others that I want to emulate in myself. Qualities such as kindness, truthfulness, generosity, and humility, which I have witnessed, for example, in my uncle, who chooses his words carefully with precision, avoids mechanical phrases, and speaks truthfully and honestly. Qualities such as self-control, courage, straightforwardness, peacefulness, compassion to all, and bountiful energy were qualities I witnessed in my teachers at the Ashram. They responded clearly to what was happening around them with poise and calm because they had healed and learned to control their minds. They

---

21 David Hawkins, *Transcending the Levels of Consciousness, the Stairway to Enlightenment*, (Sedona, AZ, Veritas Publishing, 2006), 180.
22 Swami Sivananda, *Sure Ways for Success in Life and God Realization*, (Uttarakhand, Himalayas, The Divine Life Society, 1936).

cultivated these qualities over time by living in a like-minded community committed to building character providing role models and mirrors for each other.

Thought leaders such as Joe Dispenza and Jordan Peterson have become popular because they represent the ethical and spiritual ideals we seek in our society. Peterson represents a human male ideal who reflects traditional values such as self-responsibility, authenticity, straightforwardness, boldness, and courage that people worldwide look up to yet are sadly bereft in our political and other institutional leaders. I have been fortunate to have been surrounded by leaders in the educational field who reflected these high-minded qualities. All of my instructors from my master's studies in education were profound in their mastery of their field, and after being in their midst, I was a different person.

Our environment as children informs our character, and we cannot control this, but as adults, we can. We surround ourselves with high-minded individuals and spiritual thought leaders teaching moral principles that elevate our souls. Our environment has the power to influence us so we need to discern what we will accept into our lives, so it is vital to clarify what qualities we want to cultivate in ourselves, and what we want to let go.

When we do not measure up to our ideals for ourselves, life will give us opportunities to learn, and sometimes, with a kick in the pants, we go through the fire. In my experience, the emotion of fear was causing conflict in my life, resulting in telling lies through omission and pretense in the hope it would protect me from criticism and judgment and the resulting anger that had built up over time due to this inauthentic approach to life. The fire to help me out of this prison was a conflict exposing my timid self. Looking back, I am grateful for the fire I went through today, but if you asked me then if I wanted to go through it, I would have said, "No way!". My choice of living in the community gave me no backdoor but to face myself and, with the determination needed to stick with it. The experience gave me a new understanding and compassion for myself.

Conflict arose in our community of yoga teachers in Calgary due to strong personalities, forceful self-wills, heated emotions, and differing visions for the yoga center. As a leader, I was unprepared to manage the flaring emotional reactions. Instead, I participated with a defensive attitude, the other side of the coin of offensive, with aggressive and punishing behaviors, destructive to the harmony and cohesion of the community. I had not learned how to manage my emotional reaction to the criticism and judgment of my leadership. I was stubborn and blind to my contribution to the conflict, projecting blame. In fear of being criticized, I was indirect in my communication and then, in my frustration, came down hard with an iron fist.

The Calgary centre of teachers went to the Ashram that summer for teacher training, and while on the course together, the group issues arose. My cowardly response was to avoid it and pretend everything was okay instead of addressing the elephant in the room. I was terrified of being seen as less than perfect in the eyes of the broader community of teachers, and believed I could hide from it while it was glaringly apparent to everyone.

Then, the sword of discrimination and compassion was unsheathed. The Ashram leadership called us into a meeting with the Sanyasins, a circle of wise women who gathered around me while I sat on the hot seat, facing the heat of the summer sun. I sat there hot and perspiring under the scrutiny of the wise and compassionate. Amid it, I felt like I was sitting in the Inquisition, but later, when I saw it from a broader perspective, it was one of the greatest gifts of my life, the fierce power of compassion that risks not being "nice." The questions and dialogue helped me become aware of the emotions blocking the light of awareness, the fear, resentment, and my judgment and criticism that was blinding me. It was a transformative experience, and with deep reflection afterward, I could see with the eyes of compassion for myself and my colleagues. I received an exquisite pearl of insight; I was recreating a familial dynamic of the critical, angry mother and the fearful, withdrawing father who left because he would not confront his and my mother's negative emotions. I was different; I stayed and faced it and got a special gift of insight that I would never have received if I had left.

This story reflects our tendencies to avoid difficult emotions that are the lead waiting to transmute into gold. We begin by reflecting on our emotions, which, like rain clouds, hide the sun of our awareness. We take an interest in ourselves and observe where habitual emotions such as fear, criticism, judgment, anger, and sadness arise. Due to impatience, I find myself criticizing slow drivers, and using my awareness of this habit, I stop and replace it with understanding. I feel the grip of the habit release, and I notice my body relaxing. We become aware of criticizing our loved ones, friends, and colleagues both vocally and inwardly judging them. They will feel it, and we begin to notice how they pull away, and then we criticize them for this! This endless cycle damages our relationships, pushing our dearest away. Using awareness, we practice replacing the emotion of criticism with its opposite, such as acceptance, love, or compassion. You give energy to your ideal by wanting to change the emotional habit and recognizing how it hurts you and those around you. You can use the power of intention by affirming, "I am at peace with this situation, and I bring love to all involved," and repeat to yourself when anger or impatience arises. We make an honest assessment about our relationships, observing the telltale signs of repetitive emotions erupting, suggesting a boundary breach, and call for action. When we recognize the signs of a boundary breech, take action, and bring the interaction into the light of your and others awareness. The practice of Non-Violent Communication, developed by Marshall Rosenberg, is an effective and compassionate way of sharing our needs and feelings, and setting the clear expectations for how we want to be treated. His website provides a valuable list of feelings that most of us are unaware of as we have not been educated in the language of the emotions and the needs we are blind to that to our surprise we all have.

One of the most challenging and insidious emotions is the feeling of overwhelm, the result of an overactive imagination, resulting in procrastination. Our minds are sneaky in creating 'delay tactics,' putting off our responsibilities and tasks into the future, such as, "I will do it tomorrow," or choosing intentional blindness to avoid taking action or making decisions.[23] It catches up with us, such as a bill payment or assignment, studying for an exam, or deciding to take a holiday. How can we remain aware of this challenging habit? It can start with managing your time.

Master your Emotions

- Emotions acts as a barometer of our unhealed childhood wounds.
- Accepting and exploring the root of our mental-emotional reactions is the path to self-awareness and healing.
- Emotions are clues to the state of our relationships, revealing how we are treated and whether our needs are respected.
- Emotions are accompanied by imagination, which feeds the emotional reaction.
- To heal, stay with the emotion, but get rid of the imagined story.

---

23 Swami Sivananda Radha, *Kundalini Yoga for the West, A Fountain of Character Building Courage and Awareness*, (Kootenay Bay, BC, Timeless Books, 1993), 141

Chapter 13
Time: Past, Present, and Future

"Time is an illusion."
— ALBERT EINSTEIN

How do we master time? Most of us believe we are a victim of time and that it is out of our hands and control. We either long for more time in the day or kill it with mindless activities simply to get us through the day. Alice in the movie *Through the Looking Glass* races against time, trying to change the past to save her beloved friend, the quirky Mad Hatter in the present. Time is the enemy trying to stop her from altering the past, upsetting the balance of the present. Alice realizes her folly, returns what is not hers, the ability to change the past but to learn from it, and thus makes friends with time.

Often, we live in our past, ruminating with some vain hope we can change it, imagining a different outcome. Yet, we can learn from this by using the past to highlight the needed change and applying it to the present moment of our life experience. Writing down your experience of a past conflictual event is essential to get more clarity about your actions and words, and the changes or actions needed for a more harmonious outcome.

The same applies to the future, which when accompanied by the imaginings of a future built on fantasy, results in the fight between hope and fear, pulling us into an endless tug of war. The most debilitating use of the imagination in future thinking is the habit of catastrophe thinking, creating scenarios, and imagining the worst outcomes. Replace this habit of the mind with imagining what you want, your ideal outcome! Otherwise, the mind keeps you prisoner in an endless cycle of horror stories, keeping you in constant anxiety, panic, and tension as you wait for the inevitable.

In each scenario, the past, which is no longer, and the future, which has not come to pass, are illusory. We cannot occupy the past or future, yet we can this present moment, the only reality. It is a place where I can choose who I want to be with the qualities I want to bring forward. When I am relaxed during the moment, it creates the environment for listening to what I need to do, like a wizard giving me direction in my daily life. This place of silence is where I get the most insights and guidance to the questions around my life.

My experience of time is that it can go very slowly, like when I was a young woman, spending summer holidays at the lake cottage with my family, bored because I had nothing to occupy my time. Or very fast as it does in my later years with many projects and a business to run. What is your experience of time? It can slip through our fingers until suddenly we are at a crossroads in our lives where we need to make a choice, a decision to move, leave a marriage or relationship, a job, career, or business. We look back at the years we stayed when we were ready long ago to make a change; we may have regrets or deep satisfaction, grateful for our lives. We may wish we could have seen what we know now, the learning journey of trial and error. Daily reflection helps us see clearly through these various life journeys. We learn to listen for the signs that it's time to change course, and to trust the wisdom that has revealed itself to take you to your new life.

I was living in Ottawa and working for Agriculture Canada. It was a rich time of relationships and friendship when I was blooming in my work, initiating new research projects alongside a highly supportive colleague and supervisor who encouraged me and provided numerous opportunities for professional development. I reached a peak in my career when collaborating with labs across the province, where I demonstrated to the research community the first transformation of alfalfa within the department, while writing and publishing a biological profile for soybeans. I was soaring, but my paid contract was ending, and I grew disenchanted with the world of biotechnology. I awoke one morning with an epiphany,' it is time to go and move to Calgary!' The signs were clear: friendships shifting and falling away, and a relationship riddled with challenges and no hope for a long-term committed partnership. I decided to leave with a knowing in my heart another life was waiting for me.

We are given a time limit in this lifetime. What if you gave yourself a second chance? A video I have seen on social media starts with the announcement that you have died while an image of the earth pans away. But wait! You have a second chance, a rebirth, and the world comes back into view. What would you do if you had one year to live, or one day, or one hour? Our awareness becomes laser-focused, and the true meaning of our lives, what makes it worth living, comes into sharp view. Reflect on this, and you will suddenly know what is of value and essential to you. Now you are clear about where you want to direct your attention, desires, will, and energy.

When my mother came to Calgary a few years ago, I knew it would change my life. I committed to serving her, being present, caring, attentive, and loving her in the last years of her life. I never wasted time wondering what I would do with my spare time; it was clear I wanted to be wholeheartedly with her, to share our time and love with each other. It was a great gift, and I lived at ease with the clarity and knowing I was fulfilling my purpose as her caregiver for a brief time. I now understand when they say if you need something done, give it to the busiest person in the room!

Who or what needs your attention? Can you create the time to attend to this? Plan your day based on the steps you need to take to fulfill a creative project, a new self-image, a partnership, a new career, or another. We can see what is required when we write down our planned steps. We are more precise in planning, freeing our minds from the "what ifs" because we now have a concrete plan. The step-by-step plan also helps us to avoid procrastination by removing the feeling of being overwhelmed by an unknown outcome into knowable, realistic steps that will eventually get us to where we want to go. Remember, every great adventure begins with the courage to take a small leap.

Master Time

- The only place in time that is real is this present moment
- Living in the past and/or future creates distressing emotions such as anxiety and depression.
- We learn from our mistakes in the past and we can project our clear vision for success into the future.
- Keep a short range in time for planning, creating small and realistic steps to get you to where you want to go.

Practice

Ask yourself: What are the signs it is time for a change in your life? Start by asking what is arising now in my life. Be honest with yourself, transparent, look at your life from an eagle's perspective, a high altitude, and see with the eyes of detachment. These are the signs that will reveal more to you.

Ask: What is your heart's desire? Once we have decided on a course of action, a new urgency arrives, a motivation, and a clarity we may not have experienced for some time. Our comfortable life keeps us stuck and puts us to sleep, but the impulse to life won't wait long to kick us out of the nest, especially if we are leaning on someone or something and not taking responsibility. Life is constantly changing, calling you each day into the new, yet many locked in the prison cells of their past refuse the call; when the new knocks on your door, open it!

What small step can you take into the unknown of your heart's desire? For example, you long for a relationship yet have not stepped into joining a club of your choosing or, volunteering for your favorite charity or starting a project you have put on the back burner for years.

Start now with one small step:

- Look at clubs that reflect your interests.

- Reach out and connect.

- Dare to commit to an afternoon of being with strangers.

You might discover the exhilaration of living dangerously outside the familiar and want more! Here, time is unnecessary; initiate NOW, and the shift will happen, and watch the process unfold effortlessly. The universe was waiting for you to say "Yes" to life; with that leap, the net is there.

Chapter 14
Will Power

The most important thing in life is to stop saying 'I wish' and start saying 'I will.'

CHARLES DICKENS

Making changes in our lives requires the fiery determination and willpower that I witnessed in my father, who, after being diagnosed with stage 4 prostate cancer, changed his diet, removed offending foods, drank pure water, and created significant new healthy habits. He was using his willpower, considered by Yogi's the King of mental powers. He had a solid purpose for getting well, and this health crisis catalyzed his clarity of what needed to change. Willpower develops over time with practice, like exercising a specific muscle. It is our best friend, yet it will feel like the enemy at first, uncomfortable, especially when we encounter temptations challenging our commitment, like the chocolate cake calling you when you are cleansing or detoxing.

When we resist repeating unhealthy, familiar patterns or habits, our willpower grows, and like working out at the gym, we gradually work our way up with the weights, staying grounded and realistic, and building upon each success. One sign of success is that we look forward to our new healthy habits because we experience more energy, clarity, and more. We want more!

When working with clients, we start by addressing the physical changes necessary to build will, beginning with a daily routine, for example, adding more water or exercise, removing sugar or gluten, and adding more organic vegetables and fruits. First, ask yourself what changes are needed to improve your physical health and well-being. Some common changes I see clients making when they start their new physical routines are more energy, motivation, clearer thinking, and focus and concentration. Then there are the changes of growing and strengthening willpower such as, increased daily productivity, a magnetic personality, sparkling and light-filled eyes and face, the power to influence others, and fearlessness! [24]

June was experiencing foggy thinking and feeling low energy. She had a habit of drinking soft drinks daily to hydrate. I suggested replacing the sugary drinks with pure filtered water, adding sea or Himalayan salt, which has a variety of minerals, and lemon, helping her to sustain hydration over the day. She used her willpower and gave up the daily colas, replaced them with water, and started to get her energy back with more clarity.

We start by building willpower and creating new healthy habits, and with success, we gradually change the mind's patterns. We choose an activity we love but have put it on the back burner. As a child, I loved being in my body, bicycling, running, and skipping, which developed as I grew up into playing sports, solo and on teams, such as track and field, volleyball, basketball, and tennis. I am a natural athlete, and it was in my cellular DNA. It was a soothing balm to my sensitivity as a child and teen growing up as I navigated my confusing world, thrown off my gravitational axis with the loss of my father. For you, it may be different; as a child, you may have found joy in reading, writing, playing an instrument, performing for others, painting or drawing, and more, so these activities may be ways for you to build willpower and feed your soul.

I've just returned from my daily run. Spring is beginning to swell with the promise of new growth. I am building more stamina, longer spurts, and run duration, yet I still feel the weight of winter in my body. How does this also affect my mind? The burden of my emotions?

Cultivating willpower is a workout for the mind and nervous system as you take charge of habitual, and compulsive and unconscious reactions. That which is unconscious is in the dark or unknown, like the dark root cellar of my childhood. When going down into it, my imagination

---

Swami Sivananda, *Sure Ways for Access in Life and God Realization*, (Uttarakhand, Himalayas, The Divine Life Society, 1936), 53.

created monsters who hid behind the stairs, the corners, and the shelves that held jars of fruit. Like the quintessential boogeyman who lives underneath the bed, we freeze with the thought of looking, peering to see what lies in the darkened space, fearing the imagined would leap out and devour us. When we start changing our habits and using our willpower, courage is needed, as we are facing the unknown, like the darkness in the root cellar. Turning the lights on helps us take that first step in moving into the unknown of a new healthy routine. My little heart would slow down when I could see the steps down to the damp, musty cellar with my mother's hand giving me strength or reaching for the light to see what was under the bed so I could fall asleep.

What light helps you face the imagined fears lurking in the unknown? What does it mean to you to turn the lights on? I will often challenge a limiting belief preventing me from moving forward. For example, I clarify whether the belief is real or imagined. I will review my resume when fear arises around an interview, building confidence, or I move my awareness into curiosity and openness, allowing for what the Divine has in store for me. Faith and trust may be the flashlight we need at the moment.

When building new routines and strengthening willpower, avoid focusing on the top of the mountain, with the dizzying heights that will send chills up the spine overwhelming you, and start with small steps that you can see in front of you. We want to see the large rocks on the path to step over easily.

We need light to climb mountains to see the terrain of our thinking, beliefs, and concepts preventing us from moving toward our vision for our lives. Human achievements in art, science, literature, and technology result from the power of attention and will. When we apply willpower to our higher ideals, we take the first step on that ladder to our vast potential. In contrast, it is the misuse of the will force to dominate harming others. It requires discernment and vigilance of where and how we apply our will to develop the latent potential for our evolution to the benefit of humankind.

A pervasive challenge to controlling our attention and focusing our willpower is that we live in a culture bombarded by distractions, desires, and obsessions outside us, threatening our world's moral and spiritual fabric. Our devices threaten the advancement of the transcendent human mind and spirit, which safeguards humanity from being overrun by selfishness. The distractions result in attraction and repulsion, and the enslaved personality is pushed and pulled every which way by the senses, bound by desires. When we focus within, will is fully activated. Observe where your attention is drawn and bring it back to focus on where you want to go, instead of where the dominant culture wants to take you. Use your newfound will to stay present, focus on one step you are taking, and move with awareness and confidence that you are growing closer to your dreams and ideals for life.

Master Yourself

- Willpower is the king of mental powers.
- Willpower is like a muscle strengthened by continual use and practice.
- Willpower is needed to control our attention, keeping it focussed on where we want to go and what we want to create in our lives.
- Clarity is needed to reveal the obstacles to our willingness to change and grow.

Practice

Start by choosing one compulsive habit, the pull toward some substance, person, food, or action where we go unconscious and bring it into awareness. The first mantra of Alcoholics Anonymous is admitting there is a problem and that it is affecting several domains of your life. Using your attention, acknowledge, for example, that social media takes up hours of your day while responsibilities to yourself and loved ones are left undone.

We start by watching the effects of the habit on our health, body, mind, and relationships. Observe with compassion, refraining from criticism and judgment. Decide that you will take one step, starting your day with an activity such as walking the dog, playing with your child without distraction, or with a Sun Salutation accompanied by a breath practice instead of checking your phone.

Other ways to develop willpower are to use a timer, the Pomodoro principle, and commit to a practice of 25 minutes of focussed attention on a project, cleaning the kitchen, creating a meal, meditation, or any activity that requires your full attention and presence. Then, take a break. This practice will help build your power of endurance by staying with one activity you may be resisting. At the same time, every fabric in your body would rather be comfy watching the latest episode of your favorite series on Netflix. When I run, I challenge myself to keep going when uncomfortable. I am pushing past my perceived limitations.

- Practice fasting for a day or patiently listening to another without interrupting, especially if it is uncomfortable.

- Be firm in facing your fears and do something you have been putting off or avoiding.

- Refrain from complaining about others, the weather, your surroundings, or the office dynamic. Instead, practice straightforward speech and address the issue at work with a difficult colleague or about your partner's annoying habit by communicating directly.

Air

As we move towards more subtle elements, like air, it becomes more challenging to grasp; it slips through our fingers without notice, like time. Nothing concrete of its presence exists except in the aftermath of a raging windstorm. The other night, a wind storm blew through, and the chair on the balcony had moved, and a plant toppled over. We witness air and its effect on the world, such as the sound and sight of rustling aspen leaves as they flicker the sun into sparkles of light.

Air is the abode of the heart, where we rise above the animal instincts of survival, greed, and selfishness, and the complicated emotions of anger and lust, where we now experience the desire for the well-being of others. As we increase our awareness of self, we are more sensitive to the subtler elements of life, feelings of love, compassion, understanding, and mercy. We lighten up and experience moments of joy and laughter, rising from the heaviness of our cares and worries of the past and future and experiencing the bliss of living in the present. We have forgiven those who have trespassed against us with moments of unconditional love for humanity.

Air can also be tricky when we confuse the cultural constructions of personal, romantic love with unconditional love. The longing for love from another may, in reality, be a reflection of the desire to love oneself, a necessary prerequisite for our outer heart connections; otherwise, it is vulnerable to codependency, seeking approval from the other for some exchange. Often, in these kinds of relationships, one or both are walking on eggshells, fearing the other will abandon the relationship. Our relationships offer opportunities for building self-awareness when we know that the other is a mirror for both our wholeness and wounding.

Another challenge of this place in our evolution is the discovery of the disconnect between the head and the heart. The intellect, without the wisdom, the feeling of care, love, and understanding, is a tyrant. When the "heart and mind are not in partnership, "... our vision, listening ability, reaction time, mental clarity, and overall sensitivity to our life experience is compromised."[25] We have grown up with the fear of experiencing life's negative emotions, pinging off the hard metallic and protective quality of the intellect so it does not penetrate and soften our hearts. It is here we begin building the bridge between the head and the heart, a road to accessing our full human experience and authentic self.

The health issues that arise are problems of the heart and circulation, the flow of life that animates our life. Grief impacts our hearts and, if not expressed, fills the areas of the lungs with tears, contributing to congestion. Isolation and loneliness due to fear of being vulnerable and open to others closes the heart. Rudolph Steiner said the heart is an organ of perception helping us understand what is happening within. "The heart is primarily that organ whose perceptible motion expresses the equilibrium between the upper and lower processes; in relation to them it is the perceptive organ that mediates between these two poles of the total human organization."[26] In the Eastern tradition of Buddhism, the heart is considered a brain. We now know that it shares the features of the brain, such as neurons, hormone production, and a larger electromagnetic field. According to recent clinical research on the brain's connection to the heart, scientists have discovered the heart has a brain independent of the one in our heads and tells the brain what to do.[27]

The Heart Math Institute studies the heart-brain connection and how it influences our perceptions, emotions, intuition, and well-being. According to their research, the ideal body condition is when it is in heart coherence or harmony and balance. My client and I experience this every time I start a session using mindful breathing practices such as 4X4 breathing. Many say that they are more focused, present in their bodies, more alert and energized, having shifted out of the stress response to

---

25 Samantha Orthlieb, *Opening the Senses of the Soul, Healing into Wholeness with Nature's Vibrational Medicine*, (Senses of the Soul, 2011), 146.
26 1. Our Spirit, "Rudolf Steiner on the Human Heart," Our Spirit, April 1, 2021, https://neoanthroposophy.com/2021/01/21/rudolf-steiner-on-the-human-heart/.
27 Doc Childre and Deborah Rozman, *Transforming Depression, The HeartMath Solution to Feeling Overwhelmed, Sad and Stressed*, (Oakland, CA, New Harbinger Publications, Inc., 2007), 43.

feelings of calm. Here in the heart, we experience balance and poise, responding instead of reacting to life's unexpected challenges and events. The breath and the heart work together to create a harmonious and finely tuned instrument of the body and mind. So let's drop down into the heart and listen to how we are doing, our body, emotions, and feelings connecting with ourselves and then with others.

Chapter 15
Breath

Mammals can live without food for weeks, water for days, and breath for minutes. It informs life, the subtlest of the elements apart from the ether. I remember seeing my father's body after his breath and prana, life-force had left his body, and I knew he was gone. All that remained was a material form, a vehicle without his driver, his essence, which gave him qualities we knew as our father. It is the chariot that Krishna drives for our hero, Arjuna. Without the god's life-force and his horses, the five senses, the chariot is immobile and lifeless, without the power to move through daily life. Breath, the air that feeds our cells with vitality, is the oxygen that feeds our brain with health, transforms stress into calm, and negative, weak emotions into a fuel we can harvest for our wellbeing. Conscious awareness of breath is the most critical practice for focusing and concentrating, deep relaxation, and managing the emotions that can throw us off balance. Breath provides a focus for our mind to still the racing thoughts that can come from being human in a very speedy world rife with distractions. Better breathing can help us think better and feel better.

Focusing on the breath as a spiritual practice will also increase awareness. In the Buddhist tradition, the breath is a tool to still the mind in meditation, and the yogic tradition is to clear the mind and body of excess thinking. The sages of ancient India referred to the human soul as 'anu,' the one who breathes. They observed that our first act when we are born is to breathe in, and our last act at death is to breathe out! We connect with this pulse and rhythm of life and death when we follow our breath. In the Mahabharata, Dharma, the god of Truth, asks his son and righteous king, Yudhistria, what is the world's greatest wonders. Yudhistria replies, "Every day, countless lives enter into the temple of death. Yet, those who remain in this world think themselves immortal. What could be more amazing?"[28] Our breath reflects the pairs of opposites, where we live and die to each moment through the incoming and outgoing breath, surrendering one experience to the next.

---

28 Ramesh Menon, *The Mahabharata, A Modern Rendering* (New York, NY, 2006), 596

There is a direct connection between the emotions and breath. You may have noticed that when you start to feel stressed or anxious, you lose your awareness of your breath. It becomes shallow and rapid, reducing the oxygen level in the bloodstream, affecting cognition and decision-making, activating the sympathetic nervous system, and catching us in a chronic stress loop. The more we practice breath awareness, the faster we access the breath when we need it most. So, let's talk about ways of breathing to take control of the painful loop of stress.

I teach the 4X4 breath practice that the Navy Seals, an American elite fighting machine, use in battle. I add an extra count on the exhalation and then hold my breath for a second or two, which tells the nervous system to relax. It stops the sympathetic nervous system's flight-freeze reaction, shifting the entire body to rest and digest, like that feeling after a big dinner. Many clients who practice the 4X4 breath say they are more focused and concentrated on what is happening in the present moment. Now they use it before performing a task that requires a period of focused concentration.

Secondly, practice becoming a nose and belly breather. Place one hand on your chest and the other on your abdomen and inhale slowly through the nose. The core should rise as the diaphragm, the muscle at the base of the lungs, contracts, inflating the lungs with breath. Exhale slowly, counting to 5, and hold briefly, entirely expelling the stale air from the lungs by contracting the abdominal muscles. These are the most efficient and powerful breathing techniques that the yogis use, and when we slow the breath down, especially the exhalation, it stimulates the vagus nerve. The vagus nerve is a cranial nerve, a highway that travels through the body from the brain stem, to the heart, lungs, vocal cords, stomach and other organs in the abdomen, sending the message to the parasympathetic nervous system to rest and digest. To stimulate deeper states of relaxation try humming, which stimulates the vagus nerve, on the out breath.

Slowing the breath switches off the stress response, relaxes the muscles, builds heart rate coherence, and lowers the blood pressure, resulting in a feeling of calm. Always breathe through the nose to filter out dust and allergens, warming the air for the lungs to use, and releasing nitric oxide into the blood, making it easier to breathe. Mouth breathing contributes to poor sleep, sleep apnea, brain connectivity, and respiratory diseases like asthma. When we breathe through the mouth, the respiratory process is less efficient, stimulating a stress response with the message of not getting enough air.

A more advanced breathing practice from The Heartmath Institute is the *Quick Coherence Technique*: First, focus on the heart area in the center of your chest. It can be helpful to place your hand there as you maintain your focus here, beginning to breathe in and out of this space. Start by breathing in through the front of the body, exhale out behind the heart, inhale from behind, and exhale through the heart space to the front of the body, like a pendulum. By lengthening the breath to the count of 4-5, we settle more quickly into states of relaxation and calm. Finally, add a memory to your practice of a time that inspired you, when you felt deeply loved, or a feeling of deep appreciation towards another. Continue to hold this heart focus, heart breathing, and heart feeling.[29]

As you build the healthy habit of conscious and efficient breathing, you will align your heart rate with the breath, releasing endorphins important to proper brain function. We begin to feel whole, able to focus and concentrate for more extended periods, and with restful sleep and reduced stress, we access a vaster potential of the mind and body with clarity of thinking, helping us to adapt to our quickly changing world.

---

29 Doc Childre and Deborah Rozman, *Transforming Depression, The HeartMath Solution to Feeling Overwhelmed, Sad and Stressed*, (Oakland, CA, New Harbinger Publications, Inc., 2007), 50-60.

Master your Breath

- Breath is the life-force that infuses our mind and body with energy to function in our daily lives.
- Slowing the breath relaxes the body-mind, creating calmness and clarity.
- Diaphragmatic breathing is the most efficient way to inhale and exhale deeply and slowly.
- The Navy Seals are trained in breathing techniques to adapt quickly to crisis situations and to problem solve in the moment.
- Breath techniques help to slow the heart rate, creating harmony in the body-mind, reducing anxiety and depression.

Chapter 16
Clear out the Closets

"Trying to be happy by accumulating possessions is like trying to satisfy hunger by taping sandwiches all over your body."
George Carlin

In the 20 years I was involved in a spiritual community, I spent extended periods immersed in yoga. To move to a yoga community living in shared spaces, I had to let go of most of my belongings, pairing down to the essentials. This experience taught me how little I needed to live in a community and what was most valuable. My world got simpler with more time for spiritual practice and service to others, such as teaching and leading workshops, gardening, and caring for Ashram spaces, all giving my life a sense of meaning. I was learning about what was essential to my happiness, digging deep into the unconscious where I discovered and released emotional baggage. I was creating new meaning in my life, apart from the objects of the senses, by being of service to others.

I returned to the city so inspired, relieved of a burden of self-importance, self-pity, and pride replaced by a humility that was a breath of fresh air. I had more energy as I released the tethers from the past, opening up untapped sources of creative energy. I used this surge of creative energy to re-invent myself, creating a business called *Lighten Up*, a design, decluttering, and organizational service to assist people in releasing and letting go of stuff. The stuff that takes up space while serving no purpose, like outdated, broken objects or outfits that no longer fit our evolving personality. When visiting a friend in Ottawa, I walked into her neighborhood and observed that the cars were on the streets while stuff filled their garages. The storage industry in Canada is booming as people pay monthly fees to store things they don't use, broken, unwanted, all by-products of a consumer society out of control, an addictive force that is consuming our planetary resources.

So what does stuff do to our clarity? A mind filled with stuff is impossible to see clearly and depletes our energy by the negative emotions associated with the old, outdated, worn out, and no longer relevant. After living in a spiritual community, I developed an awareness of clutter in shared spaces and a sensitivity to objects that occupied my visual world. The visual distracted me, drew my attention to it, and depending on the item's purpose, it would either energize or drain me. I was aware of objects that did not have a home, littering surfaces such as counters or cupboards without a purpose. Often, these objects were not valued nor appreciated, as seen in the chaos of the space, creating a feeling of exhaustion.

In my service working with clients, I found myself stepping into a minefield of unconscious emotions, either overwhelmed due to the clutter, angry at the thought of removing the unused that held sentimental value, and sad about letting go of the outdated with all the memories associated with the boxes from the past. When I started to build organizational systems for their valued items, they began to lighten up, such as a drawer for puzzles that the family enjoyed doing together, or a method for storing herbs that was innovative and beautiful to inspire creative food preparation, or a closet now more spacious with clothes that fit aligned with the updated woman, where they created new ensembles that reflected a more mature woman. Using principles of Feng Shui, one woman, after decluttering her home spaces associated with love relationships, manifested a deeper, more harmonious relationship with her boyfriend, and they decided to move in together.

The building blocks of life are matter, which is energy (Energy=Mass x Light2), and when there is a feeling value around matter, it takes on a life of its own. When we care for things, like people, giving them value, the space brightens and lightens. Think of the man proud of his new BMW, washing and polishing it, caring for it, taking on a quality of love. We give objects our energy, and they come alive with what we give them. I have images of gods and goddesses from the Eastern traditions, the Chinese goddess Kuan Yin and Tara, the Buddhist goddess of compassion. I dust them with a special brush only for them and place them in central locations in my home to remind me of this profound quality of compassion for myself and all beings. They are the heart of my home and have a life of their own.

When we surround ourselves with objects of low value and importance, taking up our visual space, the energy is a low vibration. The things gathering dust make the room denser, holding negative energies. I often smudge my space with sage or sweet grass to remove unwanted energies, remove clothes from my closet that I no longer wear, and regularly move furniture around, giving the space new life. I do this in my kitchen, the fridge, and countertops, keeping them clear of clutter that might interfere with my creativity in the kitchen.

As I write this, I discover objects in my kitchen, like the beautiful enamel dish holding an old Hot Wheels car, an iPod, and an essential oil spray, which I have been unaware of for months! I pick them up and give them my attention, discovering the Hot Wheels car is made in England, that I can use the essential oil spray in my space and my iPod on my upcoming trip abroad. They are dusty, sitting in my kitchen, contributing to the low-grade energy of inertia that affects my food and the eating and digestion of it. I now consider having and maintaining spaces for their specific purpose. For example, I like to write in my kitchen, yet I wonder whether the energy I bring to the area must align with its purpose and function. How can we keep our spaces clear of negative energies that interfere with the room's purpose?

An excellent example of this is our bedroom! Sleep studies suggest that a cluttered bedroom can prevent the mind from relaxing, increasing anxiety and taking longer to fall asleep. When too many colors, objects, and textures accumulate in our sleep space, it is like having a loudspeaker of unconscious messages that make falling asleep difficult. It is helpful to refrain from using our bedrooms to watch television, scroll our devices, or work and study.

When clearing our spaces energetically, remove old, outdated objects, appliances, clothing, etc., which no longer serve a purpose. It could be items with memories associated with a loved one. The decluttering process removes the inner attachments where emotions are bound up, forming energetic blockages in our body and mind that prevent clear seeing, hearing, thinking, and more. When we let go of things, their accompanying attachment is released, freeing up energy to serve the world. Attachments are the distractions of the soul, and letting go of that which no longer serves nor has purpose is one of the most challenging practices, as we are sorting through and processing memories, past identities and challenges, and our emotions. Use a journal to write to assist you as you move through your home and a box of Kleenex as you honour your past and release it. When we do this we are creating space for the new, updated you, and a home aligned with your new identity.

We start small, clearing our spaces and deciding what qualities we want in our rooms to express our personalities, whether it is functional, modern, classical, cool and efficient, warm and welcoming, purposeful, inspired, and more. Start with a room or a theme like memorabilia, the refrigerator, or the entrance closet using the Pomodoro principle of short focussed sessions of time, i.e., 25 minutes and take short breaks of 5 minutes. Start small, taking steps towards creating an efficient space that saves you time, money, and energy, which adds value and meaning when we attend to the objects of our homes. Every six months, I move my office furniture to give me a new perspective on what I am creating in my business, to see with a clear vision for the future and to plan the steps in the present. I painted my office gold to reflect wealth, beauty and joy, qualities I want to create, and share with my clients. I have sculptural art and paintings to reflect my ideals of compassion, joy, resilience and wisdom. Everything is symbolic, so become aware of the symbols you use in your space and that align with who you want to be and where you want to go.

Remember your home is your sanctuary, where you relax and restore your body and mind, share meals and space with friends and family, which uplifts you, inspires you, and nourishes your life ambitions. When it is clear and shining with intention, you have a space that will reflect the new habits you want to create, such as eating healthier foods, filling the fridge with veggies and fruit, and physical exercise by setting out appropriate clothes before bed to remind you or clearing your workspaces at the end of your day, so you start the next day with a clear mind. I have created a daily ritual of cleaning the kitchen, clearing my desk, unplugging the router before bed, removing devices from my bedroom, and, most importantly, meditating, clearing my mind for a restful evening and night ahead.

Master your space

- We need less than we think, and less is more.
- Stuff and clutter sucks our energy with our attachments.
- Use your rooms for the purpose they serve.
- Decluttering is clearing the mind, releasing the past and the identities that accompany them.
- Start small, one-step-at-a-time, and use a journal to write what arises and feel the emotions.

Ether

More subtle than air is ether the penetrating presence of all things. It is beyond our limited perceptions, unseen to the human eye, but it is what all existence rests upon. The subtle energy infuses our body with a life force that animates nature and, simultaneously, transports us to higher realms of intellect and beyond to the God force balancing all things on the tip of His finger.

When on the battlefield, just before the fighting begins and when our hero is overwhelmed with doubt about his purpose, Arjuna is taken on a journey through the hearts and minds of men, the Yogic teachings of the East by his chariot driver, the Avatar Krishna. His doubt dispelled, Arjuna is granted a boon, a vision of the Godhead. Krishna reveals his true form:

"You are the light of lights, incomparable!" Cried Arjuna in ecstasy and terror verging on death. "The sun and the moon are your eyes, your face is an eternal fire whose brilliance lights the universe. The void of space between the stars is full of you. The three worlds are in awe of the Form of yours and I tremble seeing you shouldering the sky, blazing in more colors that I had dreamt could be. I see your endless mouths, dreadful with tusks, full of Time's devouring flames and I quail. Be gracious, Lord of gods, sanctuary of the galaxies!" [30]

In life, we receive a taste of the god power that infuses each cell of our bodies that is given at birth and taken away at death. It is the subtle essence of sound and the silence encoded with messages only a clairaudient can receive. It is the call of the intuitive voice so often overruled by the tyranny of the intellect, the bliss of a mind free from the barrage of thinking. The key to all our powers is the control of the mind. We achieve balance when there is the union of God's Divine energy with the Self, the masculine and feminine, intellect and intuition, and the individual and Supreme Cosmic intelligence.

---

30 Ramesh Menon, *Mahabharata, A Modern Rendering Volume 2*, (Lincoln, NE, 2006), 146

The subtle presence of consciousness is the awareness in which we know our experience. According to Rupert Spira, a British facilitator of the Direct Path teachings and the Tantric approach of Kashmir Shaivisma, consciousness is the movie's screen, but unlike the screen, which is one-dimensional, consciousness has no dimensions. So subtle is the screen that due to the limitations of our perceptions, we have fallen victim to a belief that the movie is real or that the material world is solid and, therefore, exists. How can we know this if the mind, which is consciousness, interprets our perceptions and has been trained to believe in a material world?

Curiosity about the reality of our experience was my first step on the spiritual path, and I started with myself, studying like a scientist the nature of my experience. This process was a collaboration between the intellect and intuition, the masculine and the feminine, and when they were dancing together, I experienced higher states of self-awareness. When there is an imbalance, the intellect loses touch with the heart and becomes its worst enemy, leading to destruction. It is what we are experiencing today, an almost unstoppable force of self-destruction based on the uncontrollable ego and narcissistic personalities in our money, politics, education, medicine, and science systems. The mantra of 'trust the science' or the intellect has resulted in the mistrust of science. How can one trust today's science used to enforce a belief? Science is like life in constant flux. Science can help us understand our world, but proof without a shadow of a doubt is questionable. Most historical theories are later proven erroneous as discoveries and new technology emerge. Quantum physics, through the *Observer Effect*, is one of the most contradictory premises of quantum theory, fascinating physicists and philosophers. It states that the very act of watching the observer affects the observed reality. Therefore, how can we trust science to give us "truth"?

The science of the Self is the way of the yogi. At this level of consciousness, we have gained knowledge from our experiences and an understanding of the Truth that spiritual teachers have given voice to throughout the ages. We have been on a path to liberation, freeing our minds from the merry-go-round activity of likes and dislikes, desires, etc., strengthening our intuition, refining our perceptions, and removing the clouds of emotions to our awareness. Using the practices given, we develop inner communication and intuitive perception with increasing awareness.[31] As men and women having this material and ethereal experience, we reclaim our wholeness- our hearts, feelings and emotions, intuition, and relationships. We learn how the ego can sabotage our best intentions for ourselves and our loved ones. The courageous journey through our hearts and minds, learning from the inner teacher, is the process of gaining self-mastery, the mastery of the mind.

---

31 Swami Sivananda Radha, *Kundalini Yoga or the West, A Foundation of Character Building Courage and Awareness*, (Kootenay Bay, BC, Timeless Books, 1993), 271

Chapter 17
Silence and Sound

"Listen to silence. It has much to say...the quieter you become the more you are able to hear."

Rumi

In a noisy world of cities and neighborhoods, where car traffic and alarms, and annoying barking dogs penetrates our private spaces, many seek out solitude and silence in nature's spaces far away from the cacophony of the city. We have reached a point where we are uncomfortable with silence because when we find it, our minds get louder. I notice myself these days working from home the need to fill the space of aloneness, turning to my favourite podcasters to fill the silence. As a practitioner of meditation I appreciate the emptiness of my thoughts, receiving the noises of the outer world more gracefully, yet when working, I long for the sounds of interaction and engagement. How do I find the balance between emptiness and form, silence and sound? This is the way of the spiritual aspirant. My real work is to find silence in the noise of my emotions and thoughts when something disturbs my peace.

I have a sensitivity to the noise of cars with loud mufflers, helicopters flying above and circling, and the revving engine of a Harley Davidson motorcycle outside my home. These sensitivities result from an accompanying criticism or story that informs my experience of the noise. The thought of the sound gives me agitation or frustration that I would prefer to avoid. The other side of the coin is when we become desensitized and unaware of the sounds around us, sinking into deafness to our external world. We miss the sweet call of a robin, a cricket at night, or the glee in children's voices. We become hardened to the tone of another's voice, deaf to the vibration of sound, which gives us multiple levels of information, such as layers of history or a revelation of what someone may be hiding to protect or deceive.

Our five senses need to be cleansed and refined of the layers of emotional baggage covering the true nature of our perceptions. The stories we tell ourselves about what we hear, see, feel, taste, and smell often relate to past trauma involving one or more of the five senses. An example of my experience around sound was when I was ten years old. My father called the home telephone to tell my mother he was leaving her and our family. I listened to my mother's trembling voice and words, interrupted by her sobs and tears. I was shocked and confused. Years later in a yoga workshop on the five senses, when studying hearing, we listened to various sounds, such as the crumpling of paper and the sound of people chanting OM, while one of the sounds was the high pitch ring of a telephone. Immediately, I returned to that warm summer day in my house in London, Ontario, where I heard the phone ring and my mother crying with the shock of the news that her husband was abandoning her. It unleashed a dramatic chain of events that followed, which led to a lifetime of healing.

Unconsciously, unhealed traumas and painful memories trigger our feelings and emotions. I was blessed to have this lesson, which gave me a deeper understanding of my sensitivity and reactions of criticism and judgment to ear-piercing sound. I started to focus my healing efforts on the wounds of the past and as a result, I have learned how to shift my story around noise to a more neutral perspective. I was freed from the frustration of being unable to control my environment, accepting the disturbing noises, resulting in a more peace.

True silence comes when nothing outside us can throw us off our center, where we reside in a place of ease and inner quiet as the mind slows down and the body relaxes. The most immediate action you can take to acquire this presence and serenity is to breathe in the moment with awareness. Breath, when it is long, slow, initiated from the diagram, immediately calms the body and mind while clearing the many thoughts clouding awareness. The wind moves the weather system out, bringing a high-pressure front of blue skies. Accompanied by the clarity is a deep inner silence, a profound peace that reveals the deep inner voice of our wisdom, intuition, and God-self. Now we can hear the subtle, etheric sound vibrations of the universe that is you. This growing sensitivity allows you to listen without the interference of the busy mind that block your ability for deep listening.

While in a workshop and after days of intensive yoga practices, I immediately heard a discordant vibration when listening to one of the participants share his reflections. What I heard, I suspected, was the dry intellect trying to make sense of a painful, emotional memory, deflecting it from his awareness. I asked him a penetrating question, attempting to pierce the veil of disguise. He went silent. I later reflected on my experience of using my intellect to deflect and conceal difficult emotions taught to me by my cultural and societal upbringing passed down through generations. I heard my father's voice tremble with emotion at the Thanksgiving dinner years ago when we gathered with my whole family around the dining room table. He stood to offer a toast, and I heard a beautiful, soft voice moved by the occasion, with the feeling of gratitude and love. I was astonished in that moment as I rarely heard this side of what was a sensitive man, with the soul of an artist shut down for years. Suddenly he stopped, the veil of fear silenced this resonant, open-heartedness like a trap door, suppressing his heartfelt expression. His voice reverted to an icy steeliness, and his body hardened, protecting him from his soft feminine heart. When we can hear with the clarity needed to pierce the layers of stories and past hurts, we will truly understand our loved ones with a deep compassion for their humanness.

Pratice

Get a pair of noise-canceling headphones and use them when working on a project to help maintain focus and concentration.

Go for a walk in nature and leave your playlist and phone at home! Listen for the subtle sounds around you. I remember living on the edge of Gatineau Park in Quebec and while in the woods one spring night I heard the sound of the plant life growing through the leaves left from the previous fall. Listen with awe and wonder! Practice not speaking when listening to another, and respond only when they are complete.

Can you hear the undertones of the voice, the emotions that may be arising, the intention behind their words, and the choice of words, suggesting something about them? I.e., some words suggest ideas of self-worth, such as 'just' or 'can,' the softness of a person's voice that does not want to be heard, or the loud voice that seeks dominance over another.

Master the Noise

- Silence is the sound of a quiet mind.
- Listening is silencing the mind in order to hear the one in front of you.
- Sound is vibration; trust and listen for the vibrations of your knowing.

Chapter 18
Mastering the Mind and Our Lives

"The mind is a beautiful servant but a dangerous master."

OSHO

Mindset is an established set of attitudes determined by the culture, values, worldview, and beliefs about the meaning of life. Often, we have adopted ideas and concepts that no longer serve our life goals or purpose. We decide we need to change as the choices we have made so far are not reflecting the dreams we have for ourselves. We learn we can create our lives by directing our thoughts, imagination, emotions, attention, and willpower to where we want to go, creating clarity of purpose. It is not a simple task, but it starts with building awareness and being willing to take responsibility for the construction of our lives. We free ourselves from the victim mentality, and instead of projecting our failures and mistakes in life onto our outer reality, our family, friends, or the government, we take responsibility and empower ourselves to make the changes necessary for our evolution. One of the first practices is to reflect on the current challenge in your life and decide to make the required changes. We commit to change. We become acquainted with the hidden programs - cultural and familial programming that has got us into a feedback loop of repeating patterns.

I recently worked with a coach who helped me see I was perpetuating a victim mentality in my speech and objectifying the offender. Using this awareness, I now listen to these speech habits, such as complaining about a problem in a way that gives power to the offender and consequently disempowers me. In the past, when an issue arose, I practiced writing about it in my journal to get clear and then determine the action. Yet, with years of practice, this profoundly ingrained aspect was still present. Let me illustrate this with an example of a situation in my life now.

Whenever my neighbor smokes outside on his balcony beside mine, I have a judgemental commentary, annoyed with a desire to control. The thought is, "My neighbor is so inconsiderate when he smokes knowing the second hand smoke affects my health" (objectifying and judging the man). In my mind, I have hit him with the blow of judgment and made myself a victim of secondhand smoke. When I sat and reflected on this, my first action was to connect with him, to bear witness to his humanity and, in this case, his openness and sensitivity. After speaking with him face to face and getting to know him, my perspective shifted from being a victim to understanding the challenges of someone addicted to smoking. We even problem-solved together! We agreed that I would let him know when I was on my balcony, and he would put out his cigarette or refrain until I returned indoors. I am more or less at peace with the fact that my neighbor smokes even though the smell of cigarettes enters my space. I appreciate his willingness, cooperation, and sensitivity to my concerns.

Once we have identified the issue and, if appropriate, the historical wounding and pattern of thinking, the next step is to use this awareness to control the impulse and habit, such as in the example above of my judgment and anger. True mastery is using your understanding of the undermining habit, which in most cases drains you of your precious energy, and the choice and commitment to continued self-awareness and self-control. Now, it is essential to remind you this is a practice, a process of learning, victory, and defeat, and like the waves of the ocean have their crests and valleys; it is essential to practice self-acceptance and self-compassion. Changing a habit takes at least three months of intense and committed practice. When we fail at our attempts as we will, we re-commit to our desire for clarity and freedom.

The quick-fix solutions and distractions in our world today are some of the obstacles on the path to clarity, well-being, and success in our daily lives. Working with hundreds of clients, I have discovered one of the main obstacles to self-development is the enemy of perfectionism, with all its many tentacles. Procrastination is a common offspring of perfectionism, and at the root is fear. The fear of making a mistake snowballs into fear of rejection by family, friends, and systems such as education, with the accompanying emotions of disappointment, frustration, and repressed anger or depression.

My mother grew up thinking she was hopeless in math, and when she helped me practice memorizing the multiplication tables, she was intensely critical when I made a mistake. She was projecting the trauma she experienced as a child. When she was in elementary school and attempted to solve a math problem on the board, her teacher humiliated her in front of the other children. While some may have been immune to this, it deeply affected her belief about herself, thinking she was 'dumb'! I think now of who my mother could have been if her teacher had been more sensitive and kind.

Past traumas impact our perception of ourselves and limit our evolving potential. We cut ourselves off from the adventure and the purpose of our lives due to the fear of failure. How can we truly live if we are afraid of trying something new in fear that we will fail? The accumulation of these negative past experiences dis-regulates the nervous system, embedding the belief, i.e., "I am dumb," into our cellular memory, triggering an unconscious reaction when exposed to similar events. Making mistakes is an opportunity for growth and learning, and instead of ridiculing them, we celebrate them, opening the door of our self-imposed prison cell!

Practice

Think of the opposite of self-criticism, judgment, guilt, anger, etc., and explore the root of the trigger. Often, we will discover it is a childhood wounding, the inner child that needs your attention, care, and love.

Use reflective journaling and explore creative solutions to help you to master your mind and emotions. For example, instead of isolating myself in judgment and protecting myself from the unknown neighbor, I chose to meet him eye to eye. Swami Radha reminds us, "No man is an island. The single cell of the body functions in conjunction with all the other cells, and its existence

> depends on the cooperation of all the other cells. Our self-importance makes for a separation that will only lead to isolation."[32]
>
> When you next find yourself in a reaction, reflect on and visualize an ideal response to the situation and person.

Master your Mind

- When we commit to change we are uncovering the limiting beliefs of the mind.
- Your speech reflects your limiting beliefs - listen!
- Childhood trauma is often the clue to the limiting belief or concept about yourself.
- It takes courage to change and shift out from the habits of our minds.

---

[32] Swami Sivananda Radha, *Kundalini Yoga for the West, A Foundation of Character Building Courage and Awareness*, (Kootenay Bay, BC, Timeless Books, 1993), 137

Chapter 19
Affirmations

"Intentionality fuels the master's journey. Every master is a master of vision."

GEORGE LEONARD

Affirmations or intention setting is a practice of self-mastery, using your awareness, willpower, and the power of choice to reverse the impact of negative and limiting beliefs. When there is a deeply held belief, "I am stupid," "This is too hard," or "I can't possibly go back to university because I failed the last time," we take control by creating an affirming reminder of who and what we want in our lives. We build the circumstances of our new beliefs by stating, for example, "I've got this" instead of "it is hard." I have a client who was deeply committed to this practice, writing and reading her positive affirmations daily. A few months later, she shared that the anxiety she was experiencing in school was gone! She was now calmer and more in control of challenging emotions and negative thinking. She had reprogrammed her nervous system and rewired the old beliefs into a new way of thinking that informed and changed her life as a student, resulting in a new confidence.

Many consider this practice to be ineffective because the mind resists the positive message, which reads as untrue, like 'disinformation,' making it difficult to accept what appears to be wishful thinking. The affirmation softens the negative, making the mind more pliable to change. It is like the potter's clay; we can mold it when soft, yet the form is hard when fired in the kiln of our emotions. Our emotions have strengthened and hardened many beliefs, and it will take more time, reflection, and personal healing to make the shift. We start by addressing the limiting beliefs arising in our lives and experiment with the limitless possibilities.

I once worked with a gifted intuitive massage therapist who would pick up messages when working on tight areas of my body and then share them with me. She gave me powerful visualizations and affirmations to help me soften the holding in my body, such as an old concept and belief that life is "hard." The idea came to my awareness when I was experiencing symptoms of an underactive thyroid, making it harder to think, communicate, see, and feel, resulting in storm clouds of the emotions of the mind, blocking the sun's rays. I heard myself say repeatedly, "It's too hard!". I used the affirmation she gave me in the morning and night before bed: "I am living my life with ease, grace, and glory to the Most High." The affirmation reminded me of the support I received from my Higher Self or God Self, the grace that came when I surrendered to ease while honoring and celebrating the creator of my life. I began to relax as I planted the seed of the new idea in my mind during the liminal phase between waking and sleeping when the subconscious mind is most accessible.

The subconscious mind is where our memories and experiences are stored. When receptive, the messages come in flashes of insight into consciousness through the trap door of the subconscious mind. Many stories of great scientists who work for months on a project will suddenly have a eureka or lightbulb moment, and an idea or solution dawns. It may come through a dream or image in the mind, a thought, or a movement that triggers the moment of realization. "It arranges, classifies, compares, sorts…, and will work out a proper, satisfactory solution."[33] We can program it with what we want, such as waking at a specific hour or setting out an intention or affirmation. The best time to program the mind is during the liminal phase between consciousness and sleep, and it will work for you throughout the night during sleep. The subconscious mind can change old, unhelpful habits into healthy, virtuous qualities such as fear into courage, increasing your confidence, providing solutions to problems you are struggling with, and even a new character if you are earnest. The subconscious mind is our friend and will do what we ask.[34]

We need potent statements to shake the mind out of its slumber of past

---

[33] Swami Sivananda, Sure Ways for Success in Life and God Realization, (Uttarakhand, India, The Divine Life Society, 1936), 68.
[34] Ibid.

conditioning and to get us to our destination. The fuel is essential, so imagine the feeling of your affirmation, the confidence, and the thrill of climbing the peaks of your dreams. You cannot escape the feeling as it is always a companion of thought, so use it to your benefit. Better you master your mind than the systems of our world that use it to manipulate you, as seen in the media, television, music, and movies. Become aware of negative repetitive messages, like the recurring dream trying to wake you from the barrage of subliminal and hypnotic ideas in your environment intended to put you to sleep. Self-awareness and clarity of mind will awaken you to your brilliance and divinity.

Creating Affirmations

1. Decide what you want to create in your life, how a project or a school semester unfolds, a quality you want to develop, etc. Use the positive qualities, refrain from using "not this". I.e if you want to be more joyful, do not say, "not depressed."
2. Start the affirmation with "I am" and keep it in the present moment!
3. Use feelings to energize and fuel your desire, i.e. excited, joyful, confident etc.
4. Keep the affirmation succinct, and be specific, using the SMART goal approach found in the chapter on Visioning.
5. Repeat in the morning and before bed for a month and observe what happens.

Master your Destiny

- Affirmations soften the mind to new ideas and perceptions about ourselves.
- The subconscious mind is our friend and will do what we ask.
- Feeling is the fuel of the affirmation, so use it to take-off to your desired destination.

Chapter 20
Dreaming

"Your future is shaped by your dreams, so stop wasting time and go to sleep!"

GEORGE BURNS

The dream life is like another world, and when we acquaint ourselves with this realm, it takes on a reality of its own. I remember a recurring dream of my father's house with many rooms, several hidden away through a secret staircase. I felt a dread associated with the hidden rooms, a darkness I feared, and a malevolent presence. As I began to heal from childhood wounds, facing the memories, writing about them, feeling and letting the emotions move through me, I became more curious about the rooms, finding the courage to go up the secret staircase to see what was there. When I saw the beautiful sunlit rooms, big, with beautiful furniture, I would seek them out each time I visited, longing to see them; I knew I had healed the wounds associated with my father's choices and pain. The house, for me, was a symbol of the mind, and at the back of the mind were the rooms of repressed memories. When I brought them to the surface of my awareness, the light began to flood the upper level, revealing the beauty of the spaces once occupied by the darkness of fear of the unknown.

Our dreams reveal a vast repository of memories stored in the unconscious, hidden away from awareness, yet retrievable and redeemable. Our dreaming mind provides clues to our experience of the outer world with solutions to our current problems to what needs changing to fulfill our new ideals and affirmations. They provide straightforward direction, especially when we pay attention to them, take time to write them down, explore them in a dream journal, and interpret them.

When I explored the previous dream, writing about my interpretation, I reflected on the symbolism of houses and the ones I had lived in while growing up. In this house, reminiscent of my grandparent's home, I was familiar with the room on the lower level and less so on the upper. This dream occurred when I was developing awareness, through Yogic practices, of the hidden and forgotten events playing havoc in my life. The ground floors were the lower levels of consciousness where survival instincts dominate. As my curiosity took me to the upper floors, something was pulling me to the dark, hidden vestibule leading to a staircase leading me to a higher level, where beautiful, darkened rooms awaited. The dream reveals levels of meaning: 1) the 'I' in the dream, afraid of the hidden rooms where dangers were lurking, was a message to reflect on the fear I was experiencing of the unknown in my life. 2) The unknown or dark rooms needed light and courage to reveal what was there, and 3) when I gathered the courage to climb the stairs to the unknown, to the upper-level rooms, I was given a more expansive view, a clarity that I sought in my life.

The dream still resonates in my memory and body due to the tone and strong images, the mystery and excitement of discovery, and the beauty of the gradual unfolding of my awareness and healing. Uncovering and opening the symbols of the dream is one way we cooperate and speed up our evolution. It is another symbolic journey where we are our myth-makers using the power of metaphor. The dreaming mind is like a hero's journey of the soul as it seeks higher vistas, leaving behind the mundane of our earthly existence. As we journey towards the peak of the mountain, it is helpful to lighten our baggage, letting go of what no longer resonates with our evolving soul, such as a job, relationship, addiction, dependency, or other emotional attachments. The dream message warns us of loose rock and the internal and external predators on the path.

When living in the spiritual community of the ashram, and leading teams of visitors and longer-term guests who were volunteering in housekeeping, a challenging ego aspect arose, an arrogance that was protection from low self-esteem. A dream arrived of my great uncle Ralph, who had a cantankerous character at times, especially when we were canoeing or rowing, criticizing and yelling at me for not rowing correctly. Yet he was the sweetest man, who was generous and kind-hearted. I worked with the symbol of Ralph in me, who was losing patience and criticizing the youth. The dream character reflects the dreamer, so when we encounter familiar actors, we face our personality's pleasant and not-so-nice aspects. I was facing an unfamiliar ego aspect of envy, judgment, and anger, and the dream gave me specific directions on how and what needed to change. I learned more about my unconscious beliefs and behaviors, reactions and attitudes, and how they hurt others. Living in a community and being witnessed by my peers and teachers was another pressure I needed like the polishing of a diamond or mirror of my mind so I could see more clearly, honestly, and bravely.

The dream unlocks the unconscious treasure chest of our potential, hidden in the deep recesses, making the latent power available to use and apply daily. We think we know ourselves until a crisis arrives or we suddenly react to someone or something out of the blue. We awake from a nightmare, in a sweat, or a recurring dream prompting us to reflect on ourselves and life. The dreaming mind reminds us that we are the creators of our lives, dreaming our lives into existence. When we move through life without awareness, we create our pain, yet like the dreaming mind, there is a wise one who guides us through the snakes and ladders of our lives. To bear witness to ourselves, we must slow down and listen to our dreams. We do this when we walk in nature, have tea with our journals, sit in a sacred space, close our eyes, and simply listen for that still, quiet voice of knowing who waits with open arms for our presence.

Practice

1. Decide you want to remember your dreams in the morning. Start writing them in a dream journal. Observe the feeling quality, the imagery and the key people, animals, insects, other. Start to get acquainted with your dream symbols.
2. If you have a burning question in your life, write it in your dream journal before bed and request to your subconscious mind to give you dream to help you answer it.

3. Promise you will listen for a dream and write it down upon waking or if you wake in the night.
4. Write all the details as much as you can remember. Now look for the symbolic message of the dream, use descriptive words for each of the main characters.
5. Write an inspired message from the dreaming mind and the action needed. When you take the action, your dreaming mind will trust you are listening and will continue to send you wise messages.

Master Listening to the Messages of your Dreams

- We have an inner teacher or wise one who teaches through symbol and metaphor, contacting us through our dreaming mind.
- Often difficult personality aspects are hard to see in ourselves, and the dream helps us to see them when we are blind to our egos.
- When we apply our insights from the dream, our inner teacher takes note and responds to our questions more quickly and clearly next time.

Chapter 21
Presence

"Your true home is in the here and the now."
THICH NHAT HANH

What does it mean to be present? When thoughts of the past and the future end, this is the true clarity we all seek: a clear vision of reality, a state of presence. Being in the present is being so entirely in the moment, in the now. We stop the monkey mind racing here and there, back to past events, ruminating as the analytical mind seeks resolution, revenge, or release. Constant regret and living in the past will often lead to depression, apathy, and inertia. Living in the future initiates either the fantasy of an imagined life with a dream lover or the anxiety and fear of the horror movie, in which our minds are hardwired to create the worst-case scenario.

This results in postponing what can be done now into the future, avoiding an imagined outcome. The past, which is no longer, and the future, which does not exist, are mind constructs that hold us prisoner in the chains of our memories and imaginations. We know that we cannot go back and change the past or occupy it in the present except in our memory. The future has yet to happen, and we spend enormous amounts of time, energy, and money anticipating, predicting, and worrying about it. We live with the discomfort of living in the dark and not knowing. When the thoughts of past regrets and wishful thinking of what will come are surrendered, we open to the present moment and receive the gift of ease and joy.

When my mother was dying, I knew I wanted to be present with her as much as possible. She was in a comma, on the precipice of life and death, so I practiced being with her fully in each moment. There is nothing like death to bring us to our knees of the present moment. I sat with her, sinking into my whole being, relaxing my focus, and returning to the moment through the breath. I held her hand, massaging her shoulders, treating her mouth and eyes that would not close due to the stroke, moving her body to more easeful positions, and reading verses she loved from the bible, whole heartedly grounded in each precious moment I had left with her. Each moment as death waited to take her away from me, I was there in the fullness of my being. The experience was profound, and I knew she was aware, though unconscious. I made a clear decision, inspired by my dreams, and took her out of the cold, clinical setting of the hospital, where I was not allowed to touch her without gloves, and brought her home to die. She died with me and my brother lying beside her, loving her and sharing our memories of a long-ago time when we were all together as a family.

The more we create spaces for our mindfulness and meditation practice, the more we experience relief from the tyranny of the mind. Daily meditation has helped me to be more fully in my body and present with what is arising. When an emotion arises, I sit with it and allow it to be without the story that goes with it. It is then free to release without holding onto a story of self-recrimination, guilt, anger, fear, liberated from the attachment to the past.

Master the NOW

- The present moment is the only reality and where peace resides.
- Our full presence is a gift to our loved ones and the world.
- Meditation practice, sitting with what is, is a practice of present moment awareness.

Practice

1. Sit with your eyes closed and watch the thoughts that pass through the doorway to your awareness, your mind. Observe closely until moments of silence arise.
2. Walking meditation: walk outside repeating Now, Now, Now, focusing your mind on your feet, feeling the sensation of walking.

Focus your mind on the breath, using the box breath technique of 4x4 inhaling and exhaling, holding on each end. Even a few seconds of no thought will relieve the mind's constant activity and accompanying tension.

Chapter 22
Commitment

Until one is committed, there is hesitancy, the chance to draw back... [but] the moment one definitely commits oneself, then providence moves too. All sorts of things occur to help one that would never otherwise have occurred. A whole stream of events issue from the decision, raising in one's favour all manner of unforeseen incidents, meetings, and material assistance which no one could have dreamed would have come their way.

WILLIAM HUTCHISON MURRAY

Commitment is the glue to what makes or breaks reaching our vision for our life, our goals, and our ideals. Commitment is a goad, like an internal coach, prompting us to move past our limiting beliefs and concepts about ourselves. We remember why we are doing a practice that may initially feel uncomfortable to the mind or body, helping us remove or soften our resistance. We remember how we felt after a great meditation, journaling, breathing practice, or a run outside barefoot on the grass. (I just returned from my weekly run on my neighborhood grassy playfield and feel renewed as I return to work.) My yoga teacher reminded me often that commitment would carry me through the challenges of being on the spiritual path, like the image conjured from the poem *Foot Prints* in the sand.

> One night, I dreamed a dream.
> As I was walking along the beach with my Lord
> Across the dark sky flashed scenes from my life.
> For each scene, I noticed two sets of footprints in the sand,
> One belonging to me and one to my Lord.
> After the last scene of my life flashed before me,
> I looked back at the footprints in the sand.
> I noticed that at many times along the path of my life,
> especially at the very lowest and saddest times,
> there was only one set of footprints.

This really troubled me, so I asked the Lord about it.
"Lord, you said once I decided to follow you,
You'd walk with me all the way.
But I noticed that during the saddest and most troublesome times of my life,
there was only one set of footprints.
I don't understand why, when I needed You the most, You would leave me."
He whispered, "My precious child, I love you and will never leave you
Never, ever, during your trials and testings.
When you saw only one set of footprints,
It was then that I carried you."[35]

When we are so committed to our ideal of personal and spiritual development, it is like the universe reaches out and offers us a big hand, giving us what we need and not always what we want.

I was living in Ottawa when I had an epiphany early one morning, "I am moving to Calgary!" So, I started to reflect on why I needed to change my life as my contract with Agriculture Canada, a relationship, and friendships were ending. I knew I needed to shake things up, and I felt that Calgary would offer me a new life. As soon as I commited to moving, the universe conspired, giving me a landing place in Kelowna, where I began my journey back to Calgary, where I was born. We had a family reunion near Ottawa, where I met my cousin from Kelowna, who offered me a temporary home while I transitioned to the West. I intuitively knew I would find work at the research station in Summerland, where my skills and training would give me a job. I visited the station and met the research director, who told me no positions with my qualifications as a biotechnologist were open at the time. I was not convinced, and I returned the next week and knocked on the doors of the scientists and soon found myself in David Lane's office, who had

---

[35] "Footprints in the Sand Poem," *Footprints in the Sand Poem - I Carried You*, accessed September 20, 2023, https://poem4today.com/footprints-poem.html.

been looking for someone with exactly my qualifications. A couple of months later, I had a condo in Peachland with views over the Okanagan Lake and a contract to work full-time at one of the most beautiful research stations in the country. I felt so blessed and cared for.

Many of us have fears about commitment, afraid we will be disappointed, betrayed, or fail, convinced by our past experience of loss, divorce or a failed relationship, and abandonment, where the idea of committing ourselves is not a consideration or option. Commitment does not ensure success, but it does give you the levity, a buoyancy of resilience that carries you over the threshold of difficulty and self-doubt. The only option is to keep moving forward. At the same time, the mind refrains from falling back into the old groves of avoidance and procrastination and, with a fiery determination, advances us forward.

There are times when we need to reconsider and reflect on our commitments and whether they need adjustment or change. Our goals may have been unrealistic or lofty, our time frame too short, or a significant life shift or event has thrown us off our trajectory. We need to adjust the plan. If it is a relationship, many factors will be involved in releasing ourselves from a commitment, such as a marriage, friendship, or business partner that no longer serves our life purpose. Some stay too long in unhealthy, energy-draining, or abusive relationships. We continually assess where we are in our lives, adjusting our promises and commitments when necessary. Reflecting regularly on significant commitments to ensure alignment with your ideals and goals for your life is a healthy step in accessing your trajectory in life. A couple I admire for their conscious relationship goes away once a year for a weekend retreat to escape from the familiar surroundings and reflect on their partnership. They are committed to being brutally honest about what is working and what is not. They come away from these weekends clearer about what they want to create in the future, both together and independently, with a renewed commitment and strength of their bond, which then reverberates into the world.

Master your Commitments

- Commitment is a power that supports our ideals and life changes.
- Commitment can be scary for many, and may need healing from past transgressions.
- When we commit to a path, the universe conspires to open the doors of opportunity.
- The universe loves leapers!

Chapter 23
Attention and Concentration

"The moment one gives close attention to anything, even a blade of grass it becomes a mysterious, awesome, indescribably magnificent world in itself."

HENRY MILLER

Attention is now a multi-billion dollar industry where many forces are vying for your awareness, so it is essential to address its importance and where we put it, as it is the first step in taking control of our minds and lives. I recently told a client that our attention is a valuable commodity, so think of the cashier ringing each minute you attend to TikTok, Facebook, Instagram, Twitter, or other online distractions. When we see it that way, we realize the money we waste, like time, on what other people say and want us to think. Paying attention is sacred as it determines whether we hit the target, miss it, or hit the bus!

> Arjuna, his brothers, and cousins are in the midst of their training to be great warriors and masters of the earth. Drona, the divinely inspired archery teacher, tests them one morning and asks them to hit a target of a bird constructed out of twigs and a stone for an eye hidden in the trees.
>
> The well-trained boys aim their arrows at the bird, but before he can release it, they first have to answer questions from Drona. He asks, "What do you see?" Each boy reports he sees the trees, the sky, the branches, their bow, etc., and as a result, is sent back without releasing their arrow. Arjuna, whose heroic ability results from laser-focused awareness, determination, and commitment to his archery, is called to the front of the class, and when asked the question, answers, the bird. Drona asks, "What part of the bird do you see?" Arjuna replies, "Only its eye." Drona replies, "Release your arrow!" Arjuna hits his target exactly where his attention is focused: the eye of the bird, while his brothers and cousins are distracted by peripheral distractions.[36]

---

36 Ramesh Menon, *The Mahabharata, Volume 1*, (Lincoln, NE, iUniverse Inc.

What we pay attention to comes into existence and, with continual attention, grows in power to hold us in chains or liberate us. Where we place our attention can direct our mind into the grooves of fantasy, hope and fear, longing, desire, and endless possibilities, depending on what we are attracted to. When our attention diverts from our intention of focusing on a project, our healthy routines, caring for our spaces, or simply being present at the moment, we build a habitual pathway of distractibility.

Many today attend to their smart devices while walking and even sitting with friends and family. I once saw a family of four sitting in a restaurant, two parents and their children all on their devices. It was a strange vision, but it was also a tragedy unfolding. Are we losing our connection to our human family, isolating ourselves in our imagined digital worlds where abstract ideas and beliefs do not have a testing ground for truth? We are now more vulnerable to external forces of authoritarianism that threaten our uniqueness, intelligence, and freedoms. We are an enslaved people in some way to our electronic devices, which draw us out of our connection with ourselves and each other, and to what is real. The digital devices now provide instant gratification, from a sexual desire to purchasing whatever we want online.

Where do your senses take you? A desire to be entertained and avoid the truth of our lives or a desire for truth? The desire for truth is a call from within and is the first step on the spiritual journey. We start with building awareness of where we habitually place our inner and outer attention. We begin to witness the waste of our precious resources in the form of time and money, like the electrical current that lights our homes, the energy that informs our lives. Energy directed is a powerful force, but it can harm or kill when allowed to spill over into what is unsuitable for us. We are at the turning point where we need the clear focus on where we want to go, and if not, life comes in and gives us the proverbial boot in the wee ass to get our attention. When you focus on a lifelong dream, an issue calling you to address, or a quality you want to develop in yourself, you initiate a powerful force where the gods are inspired to assist you. Herein lies the power of choice accompanied by willpower. When you invoke this with "I will," you tap this universal energy that belongs to all. When we ensure our intentions will benefit all, your success will be theirs, too!

Our focus and concentration are essential for success, especially if you use the 'I am' statements. Concentrating on your purpose, supported by your thoughts, feelings, and actions, will be a magnet for the power of manifestation. Use your clarity of intent to be your guiding light. Use the previous practices to discipline the mind, making it your servant and liberating you. Like the magnifying glass used to focus the sun's rays burning what is in front of it, so too can a mind of single-pointed focus and purpose to transmute your life. When we start to practice concentration, we notice the resistance that arises, but after constant and diligent practice, we want more!

To start, I suggest combining intense focus and concentration with relaxation. When we begin the practice of concentration, there is a tension, and if we follow with progressive relaxation, we are tapping the power of both. When working on an extensive writing project, like this book, I set a timer using the Pomodoro app. I focus for 25 minutes on the task at hand, followed by a 5-minute break, repeated four times, bringing in a rhythm of tension and relaxation. These are the teachings of the Jedi warrior from Star Wars, where master Yoda teaches Luke Skywalker to concentrate all his mind power while hanging upside down to lift his spaceship out of the swamp. Choose to become a Jedi warrior, then 'will it' to be. Begin by committing to practice and experimenting with the tools given here.

Practices

Choose an activity or project you need to focus your mind on, download the Pomodoro app, and commit to 25 minutes of uninterrupted flow of concentration. You will need to create an environment conducive to this, creating a distraction-free space. You can apply this to anything you do and attend fully to it. Practice being fully present with what you are doing, such as writing a course paper, washing the dishes, preparing a meal, gardening, or attending to the needs of a loved one who is ill or aged. Then, take a 5-minute break and relax without technology or the use of computers.

I experience an incredible sense of well-being, energy, happiness, and clarity when using the rhythm of focus and relaxation. I used the principle of taking breaks when working on my master's thesis. I used the Pomodoro timer for one writing day, and the other without, and the difference in my experience was striking. When I did not use the timer, I pushed through to complete my task, working for hours without breaks. At the end of the workday, I felt exhausted and unclear about what I had accomplished, resulting in frustration. By the end of 8 hours with 25 minutes of focused work and then taking a break, I was energized, joyful, with a clarity of direction.

Another practice to help slow down the mind and address compulsive thinking is to pay attention to the mind, to get to know it by watching it and then facing the repetitive concerns and fears. Set a timer to 5 minutes, sit, and watch the mind, paying close attention to what arrives and where it goes. Now, in 5 minutes, write down what you observed and experienced. Repeat the practice for a half hour and then an hour. Notice what happens to the mind after this practice of an hour and overtime of repeated practice.

I have worked with clients who committed to this practice for a month of daily mind watches, and soon after, their ideals and goals transpired. For one client who experienced social anxiety, he soon after started dating. For another, he experienced an improvement in his academic performance, going from a C student to an A, who then went on to apply for and complete his

Honour's Thesis. Each one of the clients battled the demons of anxiety, which is an unfocussed mind, and learned how to harness the scattered rays of attention and direct them toward their goals, dreams, and ideals.

Trataka is focusing the eyes on a dot or object without blinking. Yogis, who are developing intense concentration use this practice, leading to the next step of meditation. It is one of the most effective methods for controlling the mind. You can use it at any time, focusing on something specific, such as when speaking to another, listening, or walking to find a point to focus on. Start the practice for one minute, then gradually increase the time. Watch for impatience, and progressively, with steady commitment and practice, you will receive many benefits, such as improving your eyesight, increasing willpower, taming the monkey mind, and eventually, psychic powers. Train for one month and take notes at the end of each week.

Ways you can practice this:

- Place a picture of someone or something uplifting, such as if you are Christian, an image of Jesus, Buddhist, the Buddha, or Kuan Yin; or atheist, a photo of a beautiful natural object and focus the rays of your mind for 5 minutes to start. Then, build upon this, increasing the time slowly.
- Place a black dot on a piece of paper at eye level before you. Focus your eyes and try not to blink, which can be difficult if you have dry eyes, so be patient with yourself. Practice for 5 minutes and gradually increase the time.
- At night, focus on a star or the moon and focus your gaze, or towards the sky in the morning when the sun is low. You will start the day with inspiration.
- Light a candle and focus on the flame.

Other Practices

- Still the body by standing still for 3-5 minutes. Think to yourself, "Standing still, not running anywhere." Reflect on what arises.
- Choose an object and concentrate on it. For example, think of all the qualities of a chair: the materials used to construct the chair, the uprightness, the purpose, types of chairs, etc. The mind will wander, so bring it back to the focus of your attention. Jack Kornfield reminds us we are training the mind like a puppy; you would never hurt the puppy; instead, you would gently guide it back to the path ahead. When the wandering mind becomes one-pointed or single-minded, it will eventually lead to meditation, inner peace, and joy.

Practice concentration daily in your life. When we fully bring our attention to washing the dishes, cooking, and caring for a loved one, we may experience profound peace, love, and, eventually, bliss. When practicing this at Swami Radha's ashram, I was cleaning and preparing for a celebration, and at one point, I was walking on air; my step was light, and I felt so much love all around me and towards others. By bringing your full attention with reverence to what you are doing, the critical monkey mind steps back, allowing for the truth of your experience that you are not the doer, only the god in you.

Master your Attention

- Your attention is a valuable commodity. Where will you place it?
- Focussed attention brings joy and peace.
- A clear, focussed mind will take you where you direct it.
- There are many practices to strengthen focus and concentration one step at a time.

Chapter 24
Communication

Words are, of course, the most powerful drug used by mankind.
RUDYARD KIPLING

In the Yogic tradition, speech can lift us to great heights or the lowest, base instincts of self-protection, attack, greed, and shame. We each hold the key to unlock the door to worlds that are inconceivable to the mind. The key is the words we use. In my journey and investigation of the power of speech, informed by my study of the ancient spiritual texts from my teacher, Swami Radha, I have begun to see speech as a beautiful work of art or an ugly one created from a palette of endless colors. In the Eastern spiritual tradition, speech is a feminine power represented as a Goddess, the creatrix, of our world. When we discover the potential strengths of speech, realizing our incredible responsibility in what we are creating is essential, we will change our world.

In my life and service, I have become acutely aware of listening for my speech and others. One example I shared earlier is a mantra I had created from my experience of struggling with hypothyroidism's physical challenges: "It is too hard." My energy was affected by my emotions and difficulty in managing them; I was tired, and my body felt heavy from problems with digestion and assimilation. I was suddenly aware one day of the message I was giving myself, perpetuating the feeling of being a victim of hypothyroidism, creating resistance to change. We must take responsibility for our creations and their consequences, learning from our words what needs to change.

When we listen closely, our speech is a clue to what is happening for us physically, mentally, and emotionally. Practicing self-awareness of the outer audible speech, we listen to the inaudible words passing through our minds. For example, I was noticing a groove of a habit of thoughts in the morning, rehashing issues arising with people in my life, thoughts replaying on the screen of my mind. The message was I was a victim of this situation, followed by all the familiar feelings of resentment, anger, and self-defense. I saw it had become my morning routine and I needed to change it. It was not an ideal beginning to my day. Now, I start my day with a new practice of gratitude, forgiveness, visioning my perfect day, and even for the next three years, creating what I want instead of what I don't want. It is like a power drink that aids me in facing and taking action on the problems and challenges in my day.

Clear communication between ourselves and others is a powerful tool for building bridges of connection, understanding, and compassion with those in our lives- our co-workers, family, friends, and lovers. Constructive words are the building blocks to crossing over to meet the other, heart to heart, while caring for ourselves and sharing our needs and wants in the relationship. Often in my life, emotions would either block the clear and loving connection or act like a shield over my heart due to resentment, withdrawing behind a shield of bitterness, resulting in returning to the drawing board for reconstruction. We need the tools to build these bridges and instead of destroying them with our reactions, we tend to regular care of the relationship, taking responsibility for our emotional life.

Consider a few steps and practices to start your new commitment to clear and loving communication. Firstly, it starts by building awareness around our emotional triggers. One of mine was jealousy accompanied by fear of abandonment. My emotions would ignite quickly, and I would need to step back and process before telling a lover what was happening to me. I learned to take responsibility for my reactions, reflecting on what was arising or happening in the relationship to understand the trigger. It often results in the awareness I need to care for myself and love myself. After doing so, I emerge from this time of introspection clearer about my needs and wants.

Secondly, I have learned the power of a question over the years to get more information to help me understand. Often, we make assumptions about someone based on our past experiences that have nothing to do with the person in front of us. We project our historical wounds on the innocent ones, and make assumptions or jump to conclusions. We take a long, slow breath and pause as long as we need, returning to our heart center, where mercy, understanding, and love reside and emerge from the chrysalis with a new perspective.

Emotional reactions that block our hearts to clear and loving communication are often a result of unmet needs that are unclear or that we are unaware of. To love ourselves is acknowledging our basic needs for healthy, nutritious food, shelter, clean water, etc.; social needs for friendship, love, loyalty, play, fun, etc.; personal needs for self-care, meditation, quiet time in nature, and connecting with ourselves. See Mashall Rosenburg's Center for Non-Violent Communication to identify the domains of human needs and their accompanying emotions when they are met or not. [37]

Lifting our emotions to the heart, where love and understanding reside, will shift the feelings quickly. Use the hands to lift the emotional energy from the solar plexus to the heart. The hands stay above the belly button, lifting up and out from the heart in a circulation motion, transmuting the emotional energy into mercy, love, understanding, and compassion. Send it out to others, sending out love to those you live with, your neighbors, the city, and the world.

We are powerful beings, yet we have fallen into a deep slumber of forgetting who we are, like Sleeping Beauty, waiting for the prince of our self-awareness and love to awaken her to our birthright. When the two mature into their rightful sovereignty as Queen and King, energized with the creative, generative vital energies they will bring order out of chaos, peace, and calm to the realm. When the two unite, clarity and calmness are expressed through the voice that is now connected to the heart, a harmony between hemispheres of the intellect and the infinite and eternal, drawing down heaven to earth.

According to Robert Moore, an American psychoanalyst and professor of psychology and religion, when these two come from their wounded

---

[37] https://www.nonviolentcommunication.com/learn-nonviolent-communication/feelings/

selves, we either use our words to control and attack others - the tyrant, or we withdraw behind our fears, identifying with the terrified child, inflating it with paranoia, the fear that imagines the worst.[38] We are caught in an unconscious reaction, lost in the desert with no sign to return us to our hearts. The breath is critical here to return us to calm poise and order to our thinking, clearing the dark clouds and illuminating the situation to a peaceful outcome.

I write this as conflict explodes in the Middle East, both sides inflamed, blinding each one to the potential for peace and justice to reign again in the Holy Land: a universal conflict, the tyrant and the weakling battling in men's and women's hearts. Until we realize the only side to take is the one that unites the Two as One. By retrieving order from the chaos, love from hatred, and when we join as One, we save ourselves from destruction. We nourish the land with the blessings of the head and heart, the King and the Queen, united in harmony protecting all the people of the land. Using diplomacy, speaking in person and face to face, seeing our oneness in the eyes of the other, guided by wise counsel, our inner wizard, we use our words thoughtfully, creating a bridge of connection and peace.

Master your Speech

- You have the power to create through your words.
- Your words and tone are a reflection of your mind.
- We start by listening to ourselves, our emotions, using the breath to clear the clouds so we can speak from the heart (hear-t).
- A question acts as a neutral tool to create clarity, understanding, and peace.

---

[38] Robert L. Moore and Douglas Gillette, *King, Warrior, Magician, Lover: Rediscovering the Archetypes of the Mature Masculine* (San Francisco: HarperSanFrancisco, 2001).

Chapter 25
ARDR Sound Healing and Brain Balancing

"Divine sound is the cause of all manifestation. The knower of the mystery of sound knows the mystery of the whole universe."

HAZRAT INAYAT KHAN

"To enter into the initiation of sound, of vibration and mindfulness, is to take a giant step toward consciously knowing the soul...Listening, learning, study, and practice are important tools. But we need the courage to enter into ourselves with the great respect and mystery that combines the faith of a child, the abandon of a mystic, and the true wisdom of an old shaman."

DON G. CAMPBELL, THE ROAR OF SILENCE

I grew up with a bright, artistic mind with an active imagination and an ability to focus and concentrate, giving me peak moments. I was a curious child, observing, listening, tasting, smelling, and feeling the world around me, connecting with and loving nature in all her magnificent forms. I was sensitive to the wonder of her creation and had beautiful moments of awe and wonder. In my adult years, I experienced these flow states in nature, possessed by the muse of poetry, often speaking in verse. I was flowing with something beyond me, connected to a vast realm beyond my daily concerns. I felt like a channel for the cosmic energies all around me, a receiver for the frequencies of subtle energies and messages coming through my vehicle of mind, body, and heart.

The cerebrum, or forebrain, is the most advanced part of your brain, handling executive and higher functions, such as thinking, perceiving, and language. It also helps control motor functions and relay sensory data. It takes up 2/3 of your brain with two left and right hemispheres. The right hemisphere of the forebrain or cerebrum is responsible for expansive states of consciousness, emotions of joy and peace, and insight and intuition, while the left relishes in facts, figures, analysis, and planning, helping us navigate our 3-dimensional reality. I look back to my younger years and later and realize I was more at home in the right brain and the flow states of the creative muse. Yet I enjoyed investigating the natural world and studying its laws and qualities, along with mathematics and sciences.

Jill Bolte Taylor, a brain scientist, spoke about her experience of a severe hemorrhage in the left hemisphere of her brain in a Ted Talk, *A Stroke of Insight*. Suddenly, the left brain went offline, while the right hemisphere suddenly became her dominant worldview. She describes the sudden moment of right brain dominance:

> "...and at that moment, my left brain hemisphere chatter went totally silent, just like someone took a remote and pushed the mute totally silent. At first, I was shocked to find myself inside a silent mind, but then I was immediately captivated by the magnificence of the energy around me. And because I could no longer identify the boundaries of my body, I felt enormous and expansive, and I felt at one with all the energy that was, and it was beautiful there. Then, all of a sudden, my left brain hemisphere comes back online and says we've got a problem!"[39]

Her experience reflects the importance of having both hemispheres online. Much of our world's educational system emphasizes the sciences, math, technology, and engineering, all left brain disciplines that focus on analysis, fragmentation, looking for problems, and placing value on the parts over the whole. The left brain analysis is often cold and steely, detached and fragmented, connected to the past and future, memory and calculating intelligence. Bolte Taylor described her stroke experience as free from the brain chatter and 37 years of emotional baggage, free of her past and immersed in the present. When we have a balanced brain between the right brain and a wholistic view, we have more perspective, like an eagle's vision of our lives and world. We live more in awe of the grandeur and beauty of the world instead of being trapped in the minutiae of the details and parts. Operating by itself, the left brain is locked in a dark closet without the light of the right, resulting in anxiety, depression, and personality disorders.

On the other hand, right-brain dominance can get us lost in a world of illusion, daydreaming, and a loss of connection to reality. There is no

---

[39] Jill Bolte Taylor, "My Stroke of Insight," Jill Bolte Taylor: My stroke of insight | TED Talk, accessed September 20, 2023, https://www.ted.com/talks/jill_bolte_taylor_my_stroke_of_insight.

ability to translate the high altitude visioning into action, into concrete steps, broken down by the left hemisphere to create in this 3-dimensional reality. Emotion is predominant over reason and confusion over clarity. We are left with all our grand, divinely inspired ideals, impressions, and visions without the lightning rod to ground them into reality.

At the yoga study center, where I spent several years learning how to bring balance into my body and mind, we practiced karma yoga, the yoga of action. We would be assigned tasks, i.e., cleaning, clearing brush, washing dishes, cooking, transcribing audio tapes of our teachers, organizing the library, etc. These activities helped ground our learnings while in class, applying it to our practical, daily activities, helping to tether us to earth. Without it, it can lead to Icarus moments, unprepared for the opening of consciousness, our wax wings melt, and we crash into the world. We first need to be rooted in the earth before we can grow into the light of our spiritual hearts, rooted in both hemispheres of the brain where the personality and higher mind dance together. In the Bhagavad Gita, the Eastern Vedantic philosophical revelations of God, Krishna teaches his devoted shisha, or student, Arjuna:

"There is nothing in the 3 worlds O Arjuna that should be done by Me, nor is there anything unattained that should be attained, yet I engage Myself in action. For should I not ever engage Myself in action, unwearied, men would in every way follow my path, O Arjuna. These worlds would perish if I did not perform action."[40]

The balancing of the left and right hemispheres of the brain, tapping into infinite potential and wisdom, is crucial for the survival of our species and planet. The right gives us a sense of meaning in the world and a more expansive vision of possibilities, while the left activates the steps discovered through insight and intuition. One way to balance and harmonize the brain's hemispheres is with sound healing.

---

40 Swami Sivananda, *The Bhagavad Gita* (Himalayas, India, The Divine Live Society, 1995), 68.

For centuries, great wisdom traditions have practiced sound healing, and today it is experiencing a resurgence. New evidence demonstrates its' efficacy and has opened up various different applications. We are essentially energy and vibration, and the principle of sound energy medicine is that specific wavelengths and frequencies of sound can make us well or sick. The work of Dr. Emoto, who studied the effects of words on water, demonstrates the impact of vibration on our bodies, setting us up for health or disease. It starts with the words that vibrate with frequencies we use on ourselves to the energy of those around us. We are aware of when someone near us is anxious or angry, affecting the health of the home, and workplace.

Lanny Williamson is one researcher and creator of sound healing that balances the left and right hemispheres while using the healing frequencies of Solfeggio. A longtime sound engineer and recording specialist, Lanny has an ear tuned to frequency and vibration. While visiting the Egyptian pyramids, he had a profound experience. He was inspired to investigate the subtle sounds and energy frequencies and the power of vibration on the mind and body. Using orchestral music tuned to one of the Solfeggio frequencies, electromagnetic tones, and panning the sound between the left and right ears when listened to on headphones, he developed a treatment for anxiety and trauma release called ARDR (Audio Reflex Desensitization Reprocessing) brain balancing therapy. Using the EMDR model, Eye Movement Desensitization and Reprocessing, which uses the rapid movement of the eyes from left to right to reprogram the mind and body to treat trauma, ARDR brain balancing sound therapy works also to harmonize the left and right hemispheres. Using the Solfeggio frequencies, the healing balm for the mind and body, ARDR promotes harmony and health.

Solfeggio frequencies date back to ancient history and are the fundamental sounds used in both Western Christianity and Eastern Indian religions, chanted by the Gregorian Monks and in ancient Indian Sanskrit chants. The numbers: 396, 417, 528, 639, 741, and 852, provided the musical notes (i.e. Hertz frequencies) of the original Solfeggio musical scale. These were passed down to Levitical priests from ancient, pre-Egyptian mystics. Dr. Joseph Puleo, a physician and researcher, rediscovered these frequencies. They were effective in helping people come back into balance, and mental-emotional healing was improved, resulting in greater clarity. Research has since identified the harmonic relationship between the Schumann Resonance (the earth's heartbeat) and Solfeggio frequencies as they both resonate with the earth's frequencies.[41]

Nine main frequencies create physical, mental, and emotional health and well-being:

174: Helps to reduce physical, emotional, and spiritual pain, resulting in a sense of wellness and safety.

285: Works to restructure weak or damaged organs, rejuvenating the body, mind, and spirit.

396: Has beneficial effects of relieving guilt and other negative emotions such as fear.

417: Produces energy to bring positive change, moderating traumatic experiences, clearing negative influences from the past, and opening the door to communicating understanding, appreciation, and awareness.

528: Energizes and heals the body and mind, resulting in increased energy, clarity of mind, awareness, activating creativity, inner peace, and emotional clarity.

639: Enables harmonious communication, encouraging tolerance, peace, and love.

741: Aids in solving problems, improving self-expression, resulting in more precise understanding and a sound and stable life.

---

41 "Where Did Solfeggio Frequencies Come From?," Brendan Murphy, accessed September 20, 2023, https://www.brendanmurphy.global/blog/where-did-solfeggio-frequencies-come-from/.

852: Increases the ability to see through life's illusions, such as people's hidden agendas. The frequency opens up positive communication and understanding of self and others.

963: Awakens our life system to its original perfect state of wellness, associated with higher states of being and the return to Oneness, activating spiritual and emotional order. [42]

Each session uses three different compositions of Solfeggio and brain balancing accompanied by 8 minutes of Resolve, a positive, emotionally stimulating track that supports the listener in resolving the memories that may arise. In my experience using the ARDR or brain balancing therapy, I have gained more frequent moments of clarity, calm, and self-awareness. Using this awareness, I have become more attentive to my needs, i.e., my vibration after listening to a spiritual teacher vs. when I have heard a discordant piece of music or how I feel around certain situations or people, helping me discern what I let into my life. This sensitivity developed with my yogic practices of chanting and visualizing light in the body, so I was very open to the ARDR, adding another level of harmony and balance to my mind.

Practices

- As we are generally more left-brain dominant, we practice more right-brain activities that emphasize rhythm, such as dance and playing an instrument or a drum, which requires more attention from the body.
- To balance the left and right hemispheres, practice Brain GymTM, which exercises coordination between both sides of the body.
- Try a crystal sound bath or buy a tuning fork and place it on the body where you feel tension. It will create relaxation where and when needed.

---

42 Lanny Williamson, *Solice ARDR Compositional Expression Handout*.

- Try using your non-dominant hand more while writing and observe the effects.
- Use the Heartmath practice of breathing through the heart space, connecting the head and heart, left and right. Place your hand over your heart, think of someone you love, and send appreciation to the world.

Master balancing your thinking

- A balance between the left and right hemisphere of the brain gives us access to our full human potential.
- Sound therapy and brain balancing can bring harmony and balance to the two hemispheres.
- Solfeggio tones are sound frequencies used therapeutically around the world.
- ARDR Audio Reflexive therapy has the potential to clear the neural networks, excavating the past of unresolved trauma, freeing us from the limitations of beliefs and concepts.

Chapter 26
Further down the rabbit hole

"There is no spoon."

Neo in the Matrix

The willingness to be present with ourselves, emotions, feelings, and memories, finding ways to release them from the body and mind is an integral part of the journey towards wholeness and healing. The material body is mostly energy, made up of the subtle element of ether, or prana, which translates into life-force. The mind translates the subtle and our fundamental essence into a visual representation we have grown up to believe in. Physicist, mathematician, and astronomer Sir James Jeans said, "The universe looks more and more like a great thought rather than a great machine."[43] The world is constantly in flux; our thoughts, feelings, and events continuously change. Our perceptions, which receive the signals of sound, sight, taste, touch, and smell and translate them into a 3-dimensional reality, reveal each microsecond of it's unfolding, which our visual cortex cannot perceive. The mind is the director of this play, constantly creating. It is a beautiful, awesome display of light that illuminates all the colors, textures, sounds, tastes, and smells, all vibrating at different frequencies, creating the movie of our lives on the screen of our awareness, our knowing.

I remember a time in my early 30s when I became fascinated by the limitations of my perceptions and wondered what the world looked like outside my five senses. I would use my imagination to step outside myself, seeing "no thing," only emptiness. When we identify with the physical body, limited, with a border or barrier of the skin to an outside world, we are bound by the laws of a material universe to an illusion. No scientist has been able to identify or find a material world because of a limited personal frame of reference, an identity based on separation, that we are a distinct entity with all our physical, mental, and emotional characteristics.

---
[43] James Jeans Quotes. BrainyQuote.com, BrainyMedia Inc, 2023. https://www.brainyquote.com/quotes/james_jeans_177088, accessed September 20, 2023.

The Yogic teachings of Advaita, a path of non-duality, offer practices to return to our essential nature, an emptiness filled paradoxically with love, peace, and beauty. These yogic visualizations demonstrate to the mind that I have no border or limitation, no scarcity or excess, and I am eternal and infinite, with nothing to fear. I have spent a life seeking happiness in relationships, careers, travel, objects of the senses, and shopping for a new outfit in the illusory outer world. Each time, I was thrown back on myself, recognizing that what I sought was unreal, constantly changing, never the same, bound by time of endings and beginnings, and did not provide the security I longed for in this mortal coil. I began to question why I was investing my happiness in something or someone that was fleeting, like sand slipping through my fingers.

So what is it that is constant? Is there anything that stays the same? When I trace back and return to that which is always present, it is only the knowing of my experience, the awareness or consciousness of my life. It is a constant companion in my life, never changed, and has witnessed all my experiences.

Ask yourself: Are you aware of your experience in this moment? It is with that awareness with which we know the world, and it is that same consciousness where the material world forms come into existence. Rupert Spira, compares consciousness to a movie screen where all the forms come into existence, are known by it, and are made of it. We know our experience by our awareness through our perceptions, sensations, and thoughts. If we follow this reasoning and agree that it is true, then everything, every object, person, feeling, and thought, takes place in, is known by, and is made up of conscious awareness.

According to Utpaladeva, an early 10th-century teacher of Kashmir Saivaism, writes from one of his stanzas on the Recognition of God:

> "The man blinded by ignorance (Maya)"... the belief that I am a separate self, trapped in a physical body, "and bound by his actions" (karma), the belief that there is a separate self and who is the doer... "is fettered to the round of birth and death"- (attached

to the objects, people, bodies of this illusory world), "but when knowledge inspires the recognition of his divine sovereignty" - (he is consciousness) "and power" (freedom from all the attachments and accompanying emotions) "he, full of Consciousness alone, is a liberated soul."[44]

I started to listen and practice the meditations of Rupert Spira in 2020 and felt like I had gone down the rabbit hole where a new, strange, and yet familiar world existed. This world was free of fear and tension and full of peace. There was nothing to attach myself or identify with other than pure awareness, which is empty of form, color, shape, thoughts, feelings, and perceptions. It is like when we sleep at night, our bodies and minds relax, where there is no-thing to stimulate the mind chatter. As we look forward to sleep as it liberates us from our identities and creations, so too can we experience this when we meditate on awareness. It does not need to be a practice but something we awaken to in the moment, returning to the infinite and eternal nature of our awareness that is uncolored, unstained, never harmed, or lacking. This knowing or awareness is the ultimate nature of our being, like a diamond, polished with clear facets reflecting the pure light of our awareness with perfect clarity.

Practice

1. Start by coming back to awareness, asking: Am I aware that I am aware?
2. Walking meditation: Walk in the present moment, using the breath as a focus, and with each step, repeat "Now". Use your five senses to keep your mind focussed on the now. Listen for the birds, look for a specific color, smell the freshness of the mountain air, or wherever you are.

---

44 Mark S.G. Dyczkowski, *The Doctrine of Vibration, An Analysis of the Doctrines and Practices of Kashmir Shaivism* (New York, NY, State University of New York Press, 1987),17

3. Sit for 5 minutes in the morning, during the day, and the evening upon returning from work, listen for the infinite, and ask for guidance on something you are struggling with. Be specific with your question so it is clear to the Buddha mind we all share. Put into action what comes.

Connect with your true Self

- True clarity is the knowing the knowing of our awareness. We see the world as it truly is, uncoloured, unstained and pure.
- Think of awareness as the screen of a movie playing out. Focus on the screen instead of the movie - this is true clarity where wisdom arises.

Chapter 27
A new beginning

"Every new beginning comes from some other beginning's end."
SENECA

We have now arrived at the end of the beginning of a journey. I have shared my personal story as inspiration to take up and take back the hidden powers of the mind and body. It is a path for the courageous willing to risk challenging the old external authorities and internal enemies. It begins with making the necessary changes that only you can identify using the evidence of your experience in this world and applying new practices to discover the eternal and infinite presence of the conscious creator of your life. Using the awareness of this power of spirit, take back your authority and make the necessary changes for physical, mental, and emotional health and well-being. You will discover over time the abode of the heart, where peace and an infinite fountain of life force resides. Pema Chodron, an American Buddhist nun, once said that if we truly knew and understood the purpose of our lives, we would practice meditation so intensely, as if our hair was on fire. If we knew that we could create better health, heal our childhood wounds, manifest our dreams, master our minds and emotions that are running us around here and there, blind to the truth of who we are, then what else is there to do but start now? Will you take one step, daring to leap into the adventure inward to the Self? Where will you start?

The time is ripe as we move into a new age, a shift of our paradigm that we witness unfolding now before us. These unhealthy systems are reflections of ourselves, where we give our power to an external authority, allowing them to move and act without impunity. Life is waking us up to shift the projection of our authority on external systems to the inner teacher and true purpose of our lives.

I recently talked with friends about the turning points in their lives that led them to where they are now. Each one said that it was an event that threw them out of their comfort zones, where people they had relied on and trusted, external authorities of aunts, uncles, parents, and grandparents, had abandoned them, throwing them onto their own two feet. Life will throw us out of the nest when the time is ripe to fulfill our destinies, where we evolve, change, and grow. One friend said with each of these pivotal moments, she had more clarity about the situation and more awareness about herself, which continues to take her on a journey of self-discovery and growth.

The impulse of life is change, evolution, growth, maturity, and dissolution, a constant flux. When we cooperate with nature's instinct to grow and change, with the ability to respond to what is arising at the moment, we are living with an empowered vitality. We are inspired by the messages of the inner guiding spirit, providing clarity when we surrender to the currents of life. This book is a guide for that journey, and it is my wish to those inspired to enter and choose one path or chapter, when applied wholeheartedly, which will open up new pathways designed especially for you.

> "In India, it is common wisdom that the world is like a waiting room in a railway station; it is not your house. You are not going to remain in the waiting room forever. Nothing in the waiting room belongs to you — the furniture, the paintings on the wall. You use them — you see the picture, sit on the chair, and rest on the bed — but nothing belongs to you. You are just here for a few minutes or hours, then you will be gone." [45]

How will you live life in the few minutes you have? Will you live like the warrior and, at the same time, the fool, innocent and free from the programs of the past? When you do, you risk change instead of inertia and fear, the mystery instead of the known, the familiar, and the comfortable. The choice is yours to burn the torch of your life from both ends, where even a moment of intense clarity is more fulfilling than a lifetime of living in the safety of the illusion.

---

45 Osho, Courage, The Joy of Living Dangerously (New York, NY, Osho International Foundation, 1999), p. 34.

Burn like a torch, if only for an instant!

Bibliography

Burchard, Brendon. *High Performance Habits : How Extraordinary People Become That Way*. Carlsbad, California: Hay House, Inc, 2022.

Campbell, Joseph. *The Hero with a Thousand Faces. 1949. Reprint, Mumbai,* India: Yogi Impressions, May, 2017.

Childre, Doc, and Deborah Rozman. *Transforming Depression*. New Harbinger Publications, 2007.

G., Dyczkowski Mark S. *The doctrine of vibration: An analysis of the doctrines and practices of Kashmir Shaivism*. Delhi: Motilal Banarsidass, 2006.

Hawkins, David R. *Transcending the Levels of Consciousness : The Stairway to Enlightenment*. Carlsbad, California: Hay House, Inc, 2015.

James Jeans - the universe begins to look more like A... - brainyquote. Accessed September 20, 2023. https://www.brainyquote.com/quotes/james_jeans_177088.

Jill Bolte Taylor. "My Stroke of Insight." Ted.com. TED Talks, 2017. https://www.ted.com/talks/jill_bolte_taylor_my_stroke_of_insight.

John Dominic Crossan. Essential Jesus. San Francisco, Calif.: Harper San Francisco, 1996.

Menon, Ramesh. The Mahabharata, Volume 1 & 2. iUniverse, 2006.

Moore, Robert L., and Douglas Gillette. King, warrior, magician, lover: Rediscovering the archetypes of the mature masculine. San Francisco: HarperSanFrancisco, 2001.

Orthlieb, Samantha. Opening the Senses of the Soul. Canada: Senses of the Soul, 2011.

Osho. Courage. St. Martin's Griffin, 2011.

Radha, Swami Sivananda. Hatha Yoga : The Hidden Language : Symbols, Secrets & Metaphor. Kootenay Bay, B.C.: Timeless Books, 2006.

———. Kundalini Yoga for the West. Kootenay Bay, B.C.: Timeless, 2011.

Swami Sivananda. *Sure Ways for Success in Life and God-Realisation.* Uttarakhand, India: The Divine Life Society, 1994.

Frankl, Viktor. *"Why Believe in Others."* Viktor Frankl: Why believe in others | TED Talk. Accessed September 20, 2023. https://www.ted.com/talks/viktor_frankl_why_believe_in_others.

www.ingramcontent.com/pod-product-compliance
Lightning Source LLC
Chambersburg PA
CBHW031116080526
44587CB00011B/992